Embracing the Sacred Seasons of Lent and Easter

Embracing *the* Sacred Seasons *of* Lent and Easter

Daily Reflections and Prayers

Janis Yaekel

TWENTY-THIRD PUBLICATIONS
185 WILLOW STREET • PO BOX 180 • MYSTIC, CT 06355
TEL: 1-800-321-0411 • FAX: 1-800-572-0788
E-MAIL: ttpubs@aol.com • www.twentythirdpublications.com

Illustrations by Janet Sue Smith, ASC. Contact the artist at smith@adorers.org for more information about the artwork. Front cover illustration is titled *If I speak without love, I am like a soundless gong.*

Twenty-Third Publications
A Division of Bayard
185 Willow Street
P.O. Box 180
Mystic, CT 06355
(860) 536-2611 or (800) 321-0411
www.twentythirdpublications.com
ISBN:1-58595-388-1

Library of Congress Catalog Card Number: 2004114625
Printed in the U.S.A.

Contents

Introduction

We all know the importance of naming and claiming our sinfulness during the season of Lent, but why does it seem that the celebration of Easter lasts for only a day? It's like spending six weeks learning new dance steps then dancing only one time.

This book is meant to help people who are making the journey through the desert terrain of Lent, ready to dance through the celebration of all fifty days of Easter. The images of desert and dance are woven into the fabric of many of the reflections found in this book. They are images as old as humanity and rich in symbolic meaning for the pilgrim of faith.

For each day of Lent and Easter, there is a Scripture citation followed by a reflection. These reflections are meant to engage the senses and the imagination as well as the heart. Next you'll find questions for reflection to help you go deeper into the theme for the day. It is my hope that these questions will help you celebrate God's gifts while at the same time encouraging positive choices for living. Each day's reflection ends with a prayer that is meant as a springboard from which the reader can formulate his or her own personal prayer.

Beginning on page 91, you will find eight illustrations that can be used for meditation. Each focuses on a theme of Lent or of Easter, and will draw you deeper into their mysteries and promises.

Embrace the sacred seasons of Lent and Easter as you journey through the richness of Scripture, reflection, and prayer to the heart of your relationship with God.

Ash Wednesday

Now is the acceptable time; See, now is the day of salvation!

2 Corinthians 6:2

Imagine that God calls out to you, that God brushes by you and says, "It's today, today is the day salvation is going to come to you." Would you hear God? Would you stop and catch your breath and say, "Whoa! God is coming into my heart and taking up residence right now, this very minute"?

Sometimes I'm so busy I don't feel God moving in and around me. I've got so much to think about, so much to do, so many people to relate to, that unfortunately I miss the invitation to accept salvation. God is saving me, calling me, but I find it too much to believe. God wants to dance with me, but even if I hear the call, I may be afraid I don't know the steps. Maybe God will notice I'm kind of uncoordinated. I'd like to believe that God offered to teach me the dance, but my timidity doesn't let me.

On Ash Wednesday the church is saying that the call coming from God on any ordinary day of the week is quite extraordinary. On Ash Wednesday the church points out in a bold way that God wants us to join him in the dance of new life, and that right now is as good a time as any to learn the steps. Are we willing to look silly, are we willing to learn new steps, are we willing to enter the dance, or will we choose to be like the shy wallflower that only watches and dreams yet never risks becoming a participant?

Questions for Reflection

• Do I believe God is calling me to dance? Why or why not?

_____

_____

• What steps must I learn (generosity of heart, patience, silence, and so on) during Lent that will help me enter the dance more freely?

_____

_____

_____

Prayer

Lord of my Life, as I begin this lenten journey, may I believe you want me to accept your extraordinary invitation to dance with you. Lead me through the steps of salvation.

Thursday after Ash Wednesday

"If any want to become my followers, let them deny themselves and take up their cross daily and follow me. For those who want to save their life will lose it, and those who lose their life for my sake will save it." Luke 9:23–24

Yesterday Jesus invited us to dance with him the dance of salvation. We were marked with ashes yesterday to indicate that we are going to accept his invitation. Now Jesus will teach us the first steps of the dance. Yet the instructions the Dancer gives today are not the kind you would normally give to someone you cared about. The instructions are about choosing life, but the method seems pretty radical: lose your life for my sake so you can save it. This kind of instruction would make many people turn on their heels and leave.

Whether we like it or not, one thing is true of Jesus: he doesn't sugar coat the truth. He tells us right up front what to expect. If we choose life, we'll come by it the hard way, through suffering and death. As paschal people we are called to embrace suffering. We are called to let go, to shed blood, to hang upon the cross for the sake of justice and truth. We are called to die to selfishness, pride, to our own personal idols, and to our part in social sin.

Learning to dance with Jesus is nothing if not about trusting. Just as we learn that when dancing with a partner, we must relax and follow the steps of the leader, so, too, we need to relax a bit with these Scriptures and know that Jesus will support us. All we need to do is keep our eyes on him and trust, trust, trust.

Questions for Reflection

• Have I ever experienced dying that brought me new life? How was Jesus involved in the experience? How do I know it was Jesus?

_____

_____

_____

• What is blocking spiritual growth in me right now? Why is it hard to let go? What does Jesus want to say to me about it?

_____

_____

_____

Prayer

God, may I focus on you as I take these first radical steps to conversion. I believe that in your arms, I will find the strength to endure the rigors of this lenten dance in the desert.

Friday after Ash Wednesday

"Is not this the fast that I choose: to loose the bonds of injustice, to undo the thongs of the yoke, to let the oppressed go free?"   Isaiah 58:6

One exciting thing about the invitation to salvation, to dance with Jesus, is that we are offered a personal and unique relationship with God. Isaiah reminds us, however, that although we have private time with God, normally the dance God invites us to includes others. In this dance we learn to hold the hands of those around us.

In this Circle Dance of Life we need to ask others to join us, but not everyone can freely enter the dance. Some are burdened down by oppression because they have been told they are not good enough, not the right ethnic group, not the right religion, or not intelligent enough to fit in.

Isaiah tells us that our real fasting is about naming the oppressed. These persons may be coworkers, neighbors, or part of our own family. The oppression might not be obvious, especially if we are the one who is oppressing. We may need to call into question long held beliefs and attitudes about groups of people as well as individuals. The oppression may be local, national, international, or even planetary. Name it and claim it! Now, today, take a "first step" by reaching out to someone who needs an invitation to dance.

Isaiah suggests we might be surprised as we invite others to dance. We may find that someone else will offer to dance with us, to lift us from the oppression in our own lives because "your light shall break forth like the dawn, and your healing shall spring up quickly" (58:8).

Questions for Reflection

• Who am I oppressing, and why? What if I gave up oppression instead of chocolate this year?

_____

_____

_____

• How do I take part in the sins of my church, my family, my nation, my world?

_____

_____

_____

Prayer

Jesus, help me shatter oppression so I can dance freely out of love for my neighbor.

Saturday after Ash Wednesday

Jesus went out and saw a tax collector named Levi; and he said to him, "Follow me." And he got up, left everything, and followed him. **Luke 5:27–28**

This gospel scene in Luke leaves us with more questions than answers. We don't know if Jesus had met Levi before this episode, or if Levi was aware of Jesus' ministry. All we know is that he left everything to follow Jesus. So little information is given yet if we draw on our own personal relationship with Jesus, we may find we know more about this encounter than we first realize.

For both Jesus and Levi, at some deep level this call and response felt right! In the moment of encounter Jesus and Levi are communicating from the core of their souls. This was a profound experience that defied emotions and could not be rationalized. We also know that, in their own ways, both men prayed. Both men were seeking God's will. They were attentive when the Spirit spoke. Both could leap into the unknown because they *just* knew that this was the right thing to do. Since this heart knowledge comes to us through mystery, the best we can do is use metaphors to describe it: I felt it in my bones, I felt it in my gut, or to follow the call was as natural as breathing.

Perhaps Levi, known to us today as Matthew, should be the patron saint of discernment. For those seeking God's will, Matthew tells us clearly that we need openness, attentiveness, inner stillness, and great faith to hear God's voice. Matthew didn't have to figure it all out. He was comfortable enough to follow, even though he didn't know where he was being taken.

Questions for Reflection

• How open am I to listen to God's call?

_____

_____

_____

• How does my prayer prepare me to hear God's word?

_____

_____

_____

Prayer

Spirit of Love, create in me a still point at the core of my being, so I might hear your call. Let me move beyond my doubts and fears by being attentive to the yearning in my heart to follow your lead.

First Sunday of Lent

The Spirit immediately drove him out into the wilderness. He was in the wilderness forty days, tempted by Satan.

Mark 1:12–13

Hot, dry, rocky, barren deserts are a bit hard for some of us to imagine during March. Yet, while I took a walk in a nearby forest this winter, I thought about a desert. The trees were bare in this forest. For the most part vegetation lay dormant. In order to find any sign of life, I had to look under the liberal coat of leaves that had settled over the forest floor. Walking by the creek beds, I noticed that the water had a thin layer of ice, yet underneath it I could see small forms of life still swimming. I thought about what the area would look like in June, with lots of vegetation, buzzing insects, chattering birds, and barking squirrels. There would be so much to see and smell and hear, yet so much would be disguised as well. As I stood in the forest now, I could see the contour of the land. It occurred to me how much the forest in winter is like a desert. I could see so much farther; the landscape changes were well defined, and any sound of consequence caught my attention. What I saw that morning in the winter forest was the truth of that piece of land.

Jesus went into his own desert to find what was real, to discover the source of his strength. He wanted to learn how to see clearly. He went to the desert so that all the trappings could be set aside.

When everything drops away, all the glitz and glitter, the busy activities, the distractions, then we can see clearly and hear the truth about our God. Once we learn our soul-scape, we can remember it even when temptations grow up around us. We will have found our true heart's desire even in the barren loneliness of Lent.

Questions for Reflection

• What clues tell me that the voice of temptation is speaking?

_____

_____

_____

• What am I most surprised to find in my inner desert?

_____

_____

_____

Prayer

Entering my desert heart I fear that loneliness will overwhelm me, Lord. Give me the courage to wait for loneliness to be transformed into solitude, where you await me.

Monday, First Week of Lent

"Come, you that are blessed by my Father, inherit the kingdom prepared for you from the foundation of the world; for I was hungry and you gave me food, I was thirsty and you gave me something to drink." **Matthew 25:34–36**

In this gospel Jesus tells us that when we look to the needs of others, we are looking into the face of God. On the other hand, when we begin to fear we might lose time, money, or freedom, then we turn away from those in need. When fear takes over, we stand still rather than dance.

Jesus' message encourages us to be proactive. To cea
is not enough. We can't stand still, for there is nothir
in a stagnant existence. Jesus' message exhorts us to er
to grab hold of life and dance. We need not be afraid .. we don't
get it right the first time. The key is to just keep trying. To become
an accomplished dancer involves a lot of practice, and we need
time to get the hang of it. Fortunately God doesn't expect perfection.

It is not accidental that the first reading today gives us the commandments, but the "thou shalt nots" of the Old Testament can
only take us so far. They are incomplete without the proactive
stance that Jesus encourages us to take in the New Covenant.

If we fear we may not be able to dance, we need to seek encouragement and wisdom from the holy people and the mentors in our
lives. Listening to their stories and following their lead can help us
stop looking at our feet and move with the music.

Questions for Reflection

• Who are the hungry and the thirsty, as well as the sick, the naked, and the
imprisoned, in my life whom I neglect?

_____

_____

_____

• What in the readings today makes me fearful, and why? Is that good or
bad?

_____

_____

_____

Prayer

*My God, I am a good person who wants to be an alive person. Help me
to engage those around me. Lead my steps into the heart of Christian
charity, into the act of loving my neighbor.*

Tuesday, First Week of Lent

For as the rain and the snow come down from heaven, and do not return there until they have watered the earth, so shall my word be that goes out from my mouth.   Isaiah 55:10–11

One of the marvels of dance is its connection to the human spirit. Dance is the expression of that spirit, and so the movements can be as varied as the emotions a person experiences. Have you ever watched someone walking and suddenly they begin to skip? Didn't that one single step speak volumes about how the person was feeling?

This reading from Isaiah is brief, like a skip, but the process he suggests takes a long time. An image that comes to mind when I think of this reading is the *Family Circus* comic strip. Once it depicted the mother calling the little boy to wash his hands. He replied, "Ok, Mom." He went to the swing set first, then past the dog, into the front yard, and on and on. Efficient use of time wasn't his concern.

God's work in the world is not about efficiency either. God's plan is about how this work can bring about the desired results. How awesome it is to realize that through all eternity God planned that I walk this earth at just this time. Even though God called out my name billions of years ago, the route to my existence has been a long one.

As we walk this earth, we long to know how God is working in our lives. We don't always understand where we are going, and sometimes we wander in the desert for years. When we experience awe at the wonder of our journey, there might even be a skip of joy!

Questions for Reflection

• Today spend some time contemplating the truth that God has always planned, that we are each a part of earth's story.

_____

_____

_____

• Have I ever been amazed at how a prayer has been answered over a long course of time?

_____

_____

_____

Prayer

I am anxious to respond to your call, Lord, but there is so much to see and experience along the way. May I realize that through these very ordinary experiences of life, my love for you is shaped and lived out.

Wednesday, First Week of Lent

Jonah cried out, "Forty days more, and Nineveh shall be overthrown!" And the people of Nineveh believed God; they proclaimed a fast, and everyone, great and small, put on sackcloth.

Jonah 3:4–5, 7–8

Poor Jonah! Here he was walking through Nineveh and preaching repentance to a people he didn't like and whom he was sure wouldn't repent. The truth was that he hoped they wouldn't because then he could say to God, "See, I told you so. They wouldn't listen to me. Now you can destroy them."

But the people of Nineveh heard the word of God coming through the lips of Jonah and, they believed. Jonah was dumbfounded. He had traveled no more than one day into the city when everyone began to repent and do penance. Not only did the common folk understand what God was asking of them, but the king and his court believed as well. The king ordered that everyone, including the animals, should wear sackcloth and ashes, fast and pray, and seek forgiveness. Just imagine keeping your dog or cat in sackcloth and ashes.

Jonah tells us that if we are prophets of God, even reluctant ones, then the word that goes out from us will bring about God's will. When we take a prophetic stance, we need to be prepared for surprises.

When the Old Testament people dressed not only themselves in sackcloth and ashes but their beasts as well, they may have thus shown their understanding that their personal sins had communal applications as well. Changing their ways included changing how they looked at the world. They realized that their society needed conversion too. True repentance must incorporate the world.

Questions for Reflection

• How am I called to be a prophet? Am I reluctant or willing? Why?

_____

_____

_____

• What does repentance mean for me in a practical way?

_____

_____

_____

Prayer

Like Jonah I too often want to judge and condemn. Help me see my neighbor's potential for glory more than their failings. May I become more conscious of how my actions contribute to the sins of the world.

Thursday, First Week of Lent

Jesus said to his disciples: "Ask, and it will be given you; search, and you will find; knock, and the door will be opened for you."

Matthew 7:7

Christians, by their very nature, are seekers. We look for direction, for fulfillment, and for others who want to walk the road with us. At the center of our search we hope to find God. Like Percival, knight of the Round Table, we wander the paths of life seeking the Holy Grail, and we are afraid we won't know it when we see it. What happens when the door is opened, and we know that we are in the presence of God?

We've been in the desert over a week now, so this may be a good time to relax and do a little slow dancing. Jim Reeves recorded a song called, "Welcome to My World." Imagine, if you will, that Jesus is singing this love song to you. "Welcome to my world. Won't you come on in? Miracles, I guess, still happen now and then. Knock and the door will open. Seek and you shall find. Ask and it shall be given. The keys to this world are mine. I'll be waiting there with my arms unfurled."

As we dance, we might ask: where exactly is God, our partner? Perhaps God stands with arms outstretched in a sunset so brilliant that we can only stand in wonder. Maybe God welcomes us to his world when we join the dance with the homeless and neglected. Perhaps God holds us in his arms when we see with new eyes that the faith of the simple soul is every bit as powerful as the faith of the greatest theologians. When we dance with God, we are called into God's world, and what a wonderful place it is for dancing.

Questions for Reflection

• If I have just settled in for a long stay in the desert, what song would speak to me of God's presence?

_____

_____

_____

• What doors have opened unexpectedly in my search for God?

_____

_____

_____

Prayer

I believe, Lord, that you are waiting for me in every breath I take, in every person I encounter, and in every direction that I wander. Help me know how welcome I am in your world.

Friday, First Week of Lent

"So when you are offering your gift at the altar, if you remember that your brother or sister has something against you, leave your gift there before the altar and go; first be reconciled."

Matthew 5:23–24

Have you ever gone out for the day with friends, knowing there was a project you really should have completed first? On the other hand, can you remember a time when you went out with friends after you had completed your work? How much easier is it to put your whole self into enjoying the day when there are no big worries looming?

In this gospel passage from Matthew Jesus suggests that reconciliation with a neighbor is really the only business we need to be concerned with. If we took these words seriously, how many of us would have to leave church on Sunday mornings to be reconciled with our neighbor? How many of us come to worship our God knowing that not all our fences have been mended, or that we haven't tried as hard as we should to make peace with our neighbor?

Jesus taught that the basis of the Christian life is love, and reconciliation is the key element in the love that God wishes for us and from us. Jesus came into the world to suffer and die so that the human family might once again have a "right relationship" with God. Reconciliation is about going the extra mile to meet our enemy on the road. It is about letting go of hate and the desire for revenge so our gifts can be freely given. Reconciled people enter into the life of Christ without the burden of unfinished business nagging them.

Easter is about rejoicing in the reconciliation of the world to God. Will I experience an Easter free of unfinished business, or will my gifts lie at the altar because I have not been reconciled with my neighbor?

Questions for Reflection

• What has been key for me to being reconciled with my neighbor?

_____

_____

_____

• How do I delay seeking reconciliation with another?

_____

_____

_____

Prayer

Reconciliation sometimes seems a large and bitter pill to swallow. Open my heart, Lord, so you can grace me with the healing power of forgiveness.

Saturday, First Week of Lent

"I say to you, Love your enemies and pray for those who persecute you, so that you may be children of your Father in heaven; for he makes his sun rise on the evil and on the good."

Matthew 5:44–46, 48

Since September 11th, 2001, we Americans have experienced the horror of terror on our own soil. We have grieved for so many lives lost. We have listened to the tales of so many who gave their lives in an effort to save others. Now we know that we are vulnerable. Now we live with some freedoms sacrificed for security's sake. We have been angry…no, we have been furious.

In this climate Jesus tells us we must pray for our enemies. We must pray for Osama Bin Laden, for the al-Qaida terrorists, for the oppressive Taliban. We must pray for people who have caused thousands of families to deal with the loss of fathers, mothers, and children. What can Jesus be thinking!

Loving and praying for terrorists is tough. If we wonder whether we can really be sincere in our prayer for these international enemies, maybe we need to reflect on how we pray for our enemies close to home. How do we pray for those at the office who give us a hard time? How well do we pray for the neighbor or community member who spreads lies about us? How do we pray for the person who has betrayed our love?

The steps in this dance of love are demanding. We may be surprised to find that the closer we are to the other dancers, the more difficult the steps become.

Questions for Reflection

• How sincere are my prayers for my enemies? How do my prayers for my enemies correspond to my actions toward them?

_____

_____

_____

• Who are my "inner circle" enemies? Can I pray for them?

_____

_____

_____

Prayer

Lord I do not want to pray for my enemies. I think it is too much to ask. I forget how important this type of prayer is to you. Teach me once again the essential movements of the prayer of love.

Second Sunday of Lent

A cloud overshadowed them, and from the cloud there came a voice, "This is my Son, the Beloved; listen to him!" Suddenly when they looked around, they saw no one with them any more, but only Jesus. **Mark 9:7–9**

We can only imagine what kind of dance Peter, James, and John were doing. The three disciples thought this was heaven on earth. They wanted to stay. When next they looked up, Jesus was standing there alone, and everything was back to normal. Yet life would never really be normal again. Mountaintop experiences are extraordinary moments that will not allow us to go back to the way we were before.

Jesus told the disciples to keep this vision to themselves until the Son of Man is raised up. What Jesus asked of these men was very difficult. He asked them to keep that special moment contained in their own hearts. Many of us would find that a difficult thing to do, but Jesus never asks without a reason. He knew that the rest of the world was not ready to hear about such an event. Jesus also wanted his disciples to keep this experience to themselves for their own good.

When God is working within us, it is important to treasure those moments in our own sacred space. Doing so allows us, in the stillness of our souls, to encounter the unfolding of the revelation. When we share a powerful experience of God too soon or too often, the power seems to diminish. This does not mean that we cannot witness to others the marvels that God has revealed. Just as the disciples would eventually know that the time was right to share their encounters, we will know when to share the wonders God has made known to us.

Questions for Reflection

• Have I ever shared a sacred experience, then later felt that perhaps the timing hadn't been right?

_____

_____

_____

• How can a mountaintop experience such as the one described in the gospel help me through the hard times?

_____

_____

_____

Prayer

Jesus, may I patiently allow your wonders to unfold in the secret of my heart. May I proclaim your marvelous love in your time, not mine.

Monday, Second Week of Lent

Jesus said to his disciples: "Be merciful, just as your Father is merciful." **Luke 6:36**

When we want to learn a new dance, it is helpful if we first watch someone doing the dance so we can learn the steps. Then we walk through the dance so we understand the progression. Finally we put our movements to music, and work at smoothing out our halting footwork. We practice, practice, and practice. Eventually the dance just seems to flow from our spirit.

The same principles apply for the dance of compassion. When Jesus suggests that we be compassionate as his Father is compassionate, we are being invited to first see how it's done. Search Scripture, the world around you, the lives of saints and holy people, and see if you can learn something about being compassionate. Once we have at least some insight, then we begin to walk through the process ourselves. As with walking we have to find the ability inside, and then begin to use it. Learning compassion for other persons may be a difficult step, but that's why we continue to practice. Eventually it becomes easier to care, and we become one with the Spirit of compassion.

Those who seek to be compassionate will always find new challenges. As soon as we think we are good at loving, we find a new situation that forces us to begin again, to learn the steps again at a deeper level. The key is to be open to learning.

Questions for reflection

• What have I learned from Scripture about compassion? What steps have I taken as a pupil of the compassionate dance?

_____

_____

_____

• Which persons in my life have shown compassion? What can I learn from their example?

_____

_____

Prayer

I desire to enter your dance of compassion, Lord. Be patient with my faulty footwork, and encourage me to keep on trying.

Tuesday, Second Week of Lent

"The greatest among you will be your servant. All who exalt themselves will be humbled, and all who humble themselves will be exalted."   **Matthew 23:11–12**

We watch a powerful head of state standing tall, with an aura of supreme confidence surrounding him. Bands play, people cheer, and it is very evident this is a person of importance. It is also easy to pick out people in our midst who consider themselves exalted. They expect certain services to be offered to them. They make a point of letting others know how many degrees they have. They may do charitable work but often with an eye to how the activities are going to benefit them.

We can probably think of two or three people who fit this description, and it's likely we didn't include ourselves in the list. We would never act in an arrogant or conceited way. We never seek recognition for anything that we do. We might even feel that we more accurately fit the description of a "suffering" servant. We are probably a little of both.

Jesus' point is not so much who is or isn't important in the eyes of the world but that we be humble. Humility is active not passive. It is a chosen stance. Humility might best be described as the approach we take toward all of life. To be humble is a dynamic quality, and the humble servant is capable of energizing others.

Humility is about living life with a sense of awe, a sense of mystery. In humility I treat the lowliest person with the same dignity as I would anyone else because he or she is a child of God. I live a humility that speaks of God's mystery alive in all things. True humility leads to joy and hope in the hearts of our neighbors. As we experience their happiness, we see the awesome power of God revealed.

Questions for Reflection

• Do I view humility as a position of strength? Why or why not?

_____

_____

_____

• How can I see my sister and brother through the eyes of mystery?

_____

_____

_____

Prayer

Humility begins and ends with you, Lord. Help me experience the freedom and joy that comes from being your humble servant.

Wednesday, Second Week of Lent

Jesus called them to him and said, "You know that the rulers of the Gentiles lord it over them, and their great ones are tyrants over them. It will not be so among you; but whoever wishes to be great among you must be your servant." **Matthew 20:23–26**

This gospel includes the account of the mother of James and John, who asked if her sons could sit at Jesus' right and left hand. Jesus, as we know, responded that the honor was not his to give.

The story could have ended here, but the other ten were listening to this interchange between Jesus and James and John's mother. They were indignant at the two brothers for asking privileges of Jesus. The fact that they were incensed may tell us a couple of things. First, the disciples likely believed that the brothers put their mother up to asking for the honor. Otherwise they would have been indignant with the mother. Second, if we scratch the surface of "indignant," we may pick up the scent of jealousy. Rather than a vision of dancing among the disciples we have an image of schoolboys, hands in their pockets, kicking their feet in the dust.

Jesus called the men together and challenged them to see leadership with new eyes. For Jesus, leadership was always about serving others.

The apostles needed to learn and relearn this step many times over. We do too! During Lent we hear the call for service like a mantra that keeps echoing in our hearts. We can pick up the beat, and we'll find places where we need to dance.

Questions for Reflection

• Have I ever been indignant with someone or something? What was it like? Where and what did it get me?

_____

_____

_____

• What does strong leadership mean to me?

_____

_____

_____

Prayer

You have called us to service, not to privilege. You have invited us to do as you have done. Shake the scales of fear from my eyes so I can see leadership as you see it.

Thursday, Second Week of Lent

"Then, father, I beg you to send him to my father's house that he may warn them." Abraham replied, "They have Moses and the prophets; they should listen to them."   **Luke 16:27–29**

In the movie *Dead Poets Society*, Robin Williams plays the part of an English teacher. On one occasion, while looking with his students at pictures of graduating classes from years gone by, he says, "Listen, can you hear them?" As the students look on intently the teacher begins to whisper, "Carpe diem, carpe diem; seize the day."

See the possibilities. Don't let any opportunity pass.

The mission of Moses and the prophets was to tell the people that they should wake up and seize the day: don't wait until tomorrow to repent and do good. We too are called to grab this moment, to embrace the world around us. The rich man in this story obviously cared for his family, so he wasn't incapable of love. His problem was that his heart was too small. He never took in those who needed him most.

Where is that rich woman or man within, the one who loves but exclusively, the one who has gifts but doesn't share, that one who has the power to unleash the gifts in another but does not? Furthermore, because we are part of a world community, we need to look at this reading in light of our nation as well. We are a society of plenty, so how are we sharing with the nations of the world that resemble Lazarus? As we care for our own grieving and needy souls, can we widen our compassionate tents to include the wounded of the world? Carpe diem!

Questions for Reflection

• What can I do for the "Lazarus" whom I pass every day? What's my excuse for not making a difference?

_____

_____

_____

• As I reflect on my ancestors in the faith, what words do I hear in my heart?

_____

_____

_____

Prayer

Day in and day out the opportunity to love presents itself, and all too often I fail to seize the day. Lord, help me respond with your love, let me bear your graces to the world around me.

Friday, Second Week of Lent

Joseph's brothers said to one another, "Come now, let us kill him and throw him into one of the pits; then we shall see what will become of his dreams." **Genesis 37:17–20**

Essential elements in the universal appeal of this Scripture story lie in the very fact that we root for Joseph to overcome the treachery of his brothers, while at the same time we can relate to the emotions behind the brothers' actions. How very hard it must have been for Joseph's brothers to accept that they were not loved as intimately as Joseph.

To some degree or other we have all danced too close to the flames of envy and hate. We are uncomfortable in acknowledging this side of ourselves. Even the smallest sparks of jealousy can be fanned into a raging inferno, and so we are uncomfortable with Joseph's brothers. Unfortunately, if we wish to journey with our inner Joseph into the desert, we will also need to allow the brothers to come along.

The beautiful reconciliation that took place at the end of Joseph's story happened because the brothers were able to grow beyond their sin to embrace yet another favored child, Benjamin. They eventually were willing to give their own lives for the welfare of this young brother. These desert nomads were transformed once they were able to face their own sinfulness. When we honestly acknowledge in our hearts and claim our own tendencies toward sin, we can begin to dance once again and set free the technicolordreamer that resides within us.

Questions for Reflection
• Whom do I envy? How does that enslave me?

_____

_____

_____

- As I acknowledged my sinfulness, which of my dreams have been set free to be lived out?

_____

_____

_____

Prayer

At times, Lord, I make some pretty miserable choices in life. Help me grow into a person who chooses more and more often to make loving decisions, to see you more clearly in my neighbor.

Saturday, Second Week of Lent

"Quickly, bring out a robe and put it on him; put a ring on his finger and sandals on his feet. Let us eat and celebrate; for this son of mine was dead and is alive again; he was lost and is found!" **Luke 15:22–24**

We've been in the desert for over two weeks now, and with all the dancing we've been doing, we may be in need of a little rest. Now we sit on a rock and take off our dancing shoes. The shoes are filled with hot, dry sand, and our feet are blistered and bruised. Why did we even think we could learn how to dance in the first place? Even if we want to get back to the Lord of the Dance, how can we, for we are weary, lost, and it seems too far to go?

As we fix our eyes on home we soon notice that our feet are slowly improving. A little farther down the road we begin to see other dancers with worn dancing shoes. We grasp each other's hands and help each other along. The journey seems a little easier now. Finally we look down the desert highway and see in the distance the Dancer. To our amazement, he is running as fast as he can toward us.

When he reaches me, I find it difficult to look him in the eye because I am so ashamed. Before I am able to ask pardon, he is lifting me up and dancing and laughing and healing me all at the same time. He washes *my* feet and fits me with new desert dance shoes. "Rest now while I prepare a great celebration," he tells me. I can't believe it!

Later in the evening, after enjoying the wonderful celebration, I realize that this great day started with just one little step, one small change that allowed me to once again find beauty in the heart of the desert.

Questions for Reflection

• How has my desert dancing been going so far?

_____

_____

_____

• What happens when I go off and dance alone? How does it feel to come back into the company of the Dancer?

_____

_____

_____

Prayer

Father of my life, if I want to make the first step toward you it means that I must admit I cannot survive on my own. Help me let go of my pride so I might know the joy of living in your embrace.

Third Sunday of Lent

Jesus said to her, "Everyone who drinks of this water will be thirsty again. The water that I will give will become in them a spring of water gushing up to eternal life." **John 4:13–14**

In the town of Sychar, people didn't go to the well in midday because "nobody was going to be there." Only the "nobodies," the sinners of society, came out to the well at midday. That is, until Jesus came! Isn't it amazing how through one brief conversation, Jesus can turn a "nobody" into a "somebody"? Engaging this fallen woman in conversation was a waste of time. Offering her the living waters of salvation was foolish. Jesus, however, looked at this nobody coming to the well and saw possibilities.

Once this empty, lonely vessel was filled with the living water of Christ, she had the courage to declare to all the "somebodys" of the town that this Jesus could bring them salvation as well. How boldly this woman danced into this new life.

Through baptism we, too, have been given this water. It is not enough, however, to just contain it in our hearts. We are called to share this water with everyone. We are challenged to change our mindset from "nobody is there" to "someone in Christ is waiting there." Can we surprise the reclusive widow next door, the newsstand vendor, and the tattooed and pierced punk rocker with the living water of Jesus today? Can we let someone else surprise us with salvation?

Questions for Reflection
• Who are the Samaritan women that I see every day? How might I engage them in conversation?

_____

_____

- Can I imagine that I am at the well with Jesus? What might our conversation be like? What concerns about my life might he have?

_____

_____

_____

Prayer

Jesus, the next time I am in the presence of people I have judged to be insignificant, help me look more deeply and discover the living water that bubbles up in their laughter, their pain, and their untapped potential.

Monday, Third Week of Lent

"Truly I tell you, no prophet is accepted in the prophet's hometown. There were also many lepers in Israel in the time of the prophet Elisha, and none of them was cleansed except Naaman the Syrian."　　　　　　　　　　　　　　　**Luke 4:24, 27**

Prophets can be described as people who think "outside the box." He or she is not tied down to business as usual. They do not have a mainstream mentality as far as their faith is concerned. They are on fire with the creative forces of the Spirit, and they must speak or the fire will consume them.

　Jesus was, of course, the ultimate prophet. He came to throw away the old patterns and to initiate new ones. He kept the people off balance and shook up their thinking. People responded to this Jesus who offered them hope in their hopeless situations. He was able to help those who were willing to see with new eyes that life does not have to be a burden but can actually be a joy. Of course not everyone believed. Relatives, friends, and people he had worked with and prayed with for years found him too much to accept.

It is still difficult to accept the prophetic words of someone we know. Jealousy may keep us from hearing God's word through them. Protective love of our child causes us to urge them to come back home and fit in. The consequence is that in our efforts to rein in the homegrown prophet of God, we become trapped in our own small, narrow-minded boxes.

Questions for Reflection

• Who are the prophets in our church? Why do we struggle with their calls to change?

_____

_____

_____

_____

• How rigid are my beliefs? Do I need to stay in that box?

_____

_____

_____

Prayer

I am afraid, Lord, to accept the words of a prophet I might have known all my life. Give me ears to hear your word and to trust in your choice of prophets.

Tuesday, Third Week of Lent

"You wicked slave! I forgave you all that debt because you pleaded with me. Should you not have had mercy on your fellow slave, as I had mercy on you?" **Matthew 18:32–34**

The principal looks down at the fourth grader in front of him. The child has been sent to the office because of bad behavior. He watches as the child shifts from one foot to the other. Finally the principal says, "Quit dancing around now, and tell me what happened on the playground."

Unlike the child in the principal's office, who is just learning about good behavior, the servant in today's story should have known better. He had been given the wondrous gift of forgiveness. All he had to do was pass it on to the next person. Sadly, his heart wasn't big enough to share mercy with his neighbor.

God's compassionate heart is overflowing with forgiveness for those who desire it, and God is willing to do this over and over again. What God asks in return is that we get in touch with this experience of compassion deep down in our soul, to let the freedom born of God's mercy transform us. Then God asks just one more thing: that we pass this freedom along to those in need of our forgiveness.

Jesus' stern warning about the consequences of withholding our forgiveness is really to let us know how crucial this issue is in the formation of a mature Christian. If we go beyond the warning we find more; we find the rich offer to taste the power and joy of being one with God. Isn't that awesome!

Questions for Reflection

• Can I describe my most powerful experience of forgiveness? Did it empower me? Do I believe that God can forgive anything?

_____

_____

_____

• Do I believe I can forgive anything with the help of God? What steps might help me pardon another?

_____

_____

_____

Prayer

As I dance the difficult steps of forgiveness help me keep my heart focused on how I feel when I experience your pardon, Lord. Let me realize the great power unleashed in me when I pass that forgiveness on to my neighbor.

Wednesday, Third Week of Lent

Jesus said, "Do not think that I have come to abolish the law or the prophets; I have come not to abolish but to fulfill."

Matthew 5:17,19

It is hard to travel in the desert in the middle of a sandstorm. The sand blows so hard your exposed skin begins to feel like a pincushion. You can't look around for fear of getting sand in your eyes. Even if you could see, visibility is so poor that you have no sense of direction. Spiritual sandstorms are similar. There are so many different statements about laws and commands in the gospels. Some say one thing, and then another statement seems to lead us in the opposite direction. We are afraid to take a step because we don't know which is the right path.

In a desert sandstorm the best thing to do is find a rock or other sheltered area and wait out the storm. The same can be said for the spiritual storm. Hunker down in prayer, and eventually the truth will become clearer. Perhaps the first thing that surfaces is the fact that the "law" Jesus is talking about is love. Love is dynamic, so it cannot be confined to one set of rigid rules and regulations.

Jesus also tells us that he came to fulfill the law and that those of us who live the law fully will be great in the kingdom. Living the law fully means loving completely. Every other statute or code of conduct is meant to facilitate loving as Jesus would love. When we are truly focused on loving, we will find our way home.

Questions for Reflection
• How does the law of love that God encourages differ from love that depends on rigid observation of rules and regulations?

_____

_____

_____

• How do I read my heart map? What landmarks tell me if I'm on the right or wrong path?

_____

_____

_____

Prayer
Enfold me in your tent, Lord, when the storms of confusion rage around me. Enlighten my heart so I can see clearly which direction leads most surely through the deserts of doubt and uncertainty.

Thursday, Third Week of Lent

"Whoever is not with me is against me, and whoever does not gather with me scatters."   **Luke 11:23**

An ice skater puts in long days of practice to perfect her jumps and spins. Time and time again she falls, gets bruised, then pushes herself back up to start over again. Today I am trying, once again, to practice this lenten dance. These are tough days because my motivation has to come from within. Yes, I want to be the best I can be but....

Like a coach who needs to exhort her skater to decide whether she wants to be a champion or not, so too Jesus challenges his followers. In some respects this Scripture passage from Luke reminds us that we have to give our all to this journey toward salvation. We cannot vacillate. We must be committed.

We all want to be that committed, but on the hard days, the days of temptation, we realize just how much more practice we need. We hear this quote from Scripture and say, "Yes, I'm with you, Lord." We pause and then add "but...." We want to qualify our commitment. If I am out in the desert today by myself, I could skip the hard steps, couldn't I?

The middle of Lent is a tough time to make a commitment to continue the dance, but look deep inside and see who is watching this practice session. This is the One with whom you can take up the burden of perfection, who will understand just how hard it is to be with him all the time. In the presence of this One perhaps the burden can be lifted and the dance made lighter and the desire enflamed once again.

Questions for Reflection

• While dancing in the desert this Lent have I fallen?

_____

_____

_____

• Can I image Jesus as my own personal "cheerleader"? What does he want to say to me?

_____

_____

_____

Prayer

Jesus, give me the strength to keep practicing the steps of this lenten dance. May I not succumb to the desire to quit halfway through the journey. Keep me steadfast in my commitment to follow your lead always.

Friday, Third Week of Lent

Then the scribe said to him, "You are right, Teacher; you have truly said that 'he is one, and besides him there is no other.'"…When Jesus saw that he answered wisely, he said to him, "You are not far from the kingdom of God." **Mark 12:32–34**

The scribe in this gospel seems to have been searching at some deep level to really know God's will. Perhaps he prayed for clarity, for understanding the bottom line on how to live a good life. His search was so important that he was willing to risk his reputation by engaging Jesus in sincere conversation. As he listened to Jesus, he must have felt he had found a kindred spirit. Here was someone who spoke about what really mattered. The words the scribe speaks in this passage are words of excitement and sincerity. Jesus validated the scribe's insight and offered encouragement for the journey by letting him know he was close to the reign of God.

All of us need validation on our faith journey. We could not continue without encouragement. Sometimes confirmation comes directly from God when we experience peace in a turbulent situation, or when a solution to a problem suddenly becomes clear, or when we realize we have gifts we didn't know we possessed. Sometimes God gives us support through a spiritual director, a mentor, or a good and trusted friend.

The important thing is to be ready to hear the word. We need to trust our own hearts and to be honestly in touch with the fire that burns within. Then we will begin to recognize the Dancer's steps in the voices of the world around me.

Questions for Reflection

• How do I know when I have been truly inspired by God?

_____

_____

_____

_____

• In what ways has my faith been validated by a personal encounter with God or through service in God's world?

_____

_____

_____

Prayer

God, the road seems so long at times I am not sure if I am really on the right path. Bless me with more awareness of your validation of my journey because I can always use a little more spring in my step.

Saturday, Third Week of Lent

"Let us know, let us press on to know the Lord; his appearing is as sure as the dawn; he will come to us like the showers, like the spring rains that water the earth."   Hosea 6:3

On many mornings I find myself waking shortly before the dawn. What a blessing this has been for me! I often wish I could capture in watercolors the rising morning. There is something sacred about this quiet approach of the sun. Not a sound is made, yet the energy of the day is something we cannot fathom. The sounds we hear are the earth's response to the new day. I want to paint, record, or in some way hold the moment and its beauty.

Not many things are constant in life, but as long as the earth exists and as long as we live, each day there will be a dawn. When we anticipate a special day, the dawn seems to take forever to appear. During the lonely nights of great sadness, we wonder if the dawn will ever come. It always appears.

It is good to have some certainty in our lives, for so many things are uncertain. I might have the best credentials for a position, but it doesn't mean I'll get the job. The fact that I love someone does not guarantee they will love me in return. I can have all the money in the world and still not be happy. Lack of certainty is part of life.

Like the dawn, the judgment of God is a sure thing. The deepest areas of my soul will be illuminated by God's justice. All people who walk upon this earth, whether good or evil, will fall under this judgment. The question might be, "Will I be prepared to embrace *this* dawn?"

Questions for Reflection

• Looking back at the first part of Lent, what has been the most important insight I have had?

_____

_____

_____

• What things are certain in my life?

_____

_____

_____

Prayer

The dawn of your judgment, Lord, may come very silently or unexpectedly for me. May my life be a confident statement of my readiness to embrace that day.

Fourth Sunday of Lent

The man born blind said to the Pharisees, "Never since the world began has it been heard that anyone opened the eyes of a person born blind. If this man were not from God, he could do nothing." **John 9:30–33**

In John's gospel we find Jesus trying to minister in and around the temple. The tension building between Jesus and the Pharisees was the backdrop for the cure of the man born blind. The miracle was mind-boggling. This man who had never been able to see could then see clearly.

The real focus of this story is not on the man's physical blindness but on the deeper spiritual vision he possessed, which Jesus validated. The blind man had no formal education. Yet he had a natural ability to see more clearly than the learned Pharisees. This beggar's inner sight perceived the passion inside Jesus, the passion to make the broken whole. He was able to see very clearly that jealousy and envy were motivating the Pharisees.

Perhaps the "feel good" conclusion of this story comes because the insightful blind man didn't lose his inner perception simply because he had physical sight. This inner vision fed his courageous and eloquent response to the Pharisees. Later when he acclaimed Jesus as Lord, he did so because he saw clearly all the way from his heart.

Questions for Reflection

• What dream, hope, or desire inside of me needs to be set free? Will I let Jesus help?

_____

_____

_____

_____

• When I meet Pharisees in my world, what do I do to confront their message?

_____

_____

_____

Prayer

God, you have graced all of us with the ability to perceive your truth. Give us the courage to speak this truth to those who need to hear it most, and even to those who do not wish to hear it.

Monday, Fourth Week of Lent

The official said to him, "Sir, come down before my little boy dies." Jesus said to him, "Go; your son will live." The man believed the word that Jesus spoke to him and started on his way.   **John 4:49–50**

Learning to dance in the desert involves a lot of footwork, patience, practice—and trust. As my trust grows, I become more confident and can enjoy the experience more. At the beginning of this lenten dance Jesus asked us to let him lead us to a deeper relationship. He asked the same thing of the royal official. Any relationship at some point calls us to deeper trust. Our fragile faith can be fractured so badly it might seem safer to discard it, as one might amputate a useless limb.

What Jesus asked of the royal official was to believe without security. Believe even though my physical presence won't be there to give you assurance. Believe that my spoken words have the power to bring about what I desire.

Can I do this? My life has been filled with disappointments, times when my faith has been bruised and even broken. I want to believe, and at the same time I don't want to believe. I wonder if I could set out like the royal official. Could I go home if I didn't have proof that my child had been cured? Have I already given up on God? If this is my story, then perhaps I sit like an invalid unable to dance. I am yearning to step out in trust but wondering how I can. Can we pray for healing of the injuries caused when loved ones have broken trust with us? If we close our eyes, we might hear the Dancer whisper, "Gently, invalid, I will teach you once again to dance with trust."

Questions for Reflection

• What hinders me from trusting as the royal official did?

_____

_____

_____

• How have I hindered the faith of my neighbor? How can I help my neighbor regain his or her faith footing?

_____

_____

_____

Prayer

I am handicapped by a faith that too often fails to abandon itself into your embrace, Lord. During this lenten season may I leap more deeply into your love by trusting more completely in your promise to catch me.

Tuesday, Fourth Week of Lent

"See, you have been made well! Do not sin any more, so that nothing worse happens to you." John 5:14

In an earlier part of this exchange between Jesus and the sick man we find a hint of an underlying problem. Jesus asked the man if he wanted to be healed. The man replied that he could not get to the Sheep Pool on his own and no one had helped him. Rather than deal with the present possibility of a cure, he offered an excuse for not finding wellness in the past. Jesus cured him of his physical illness but told the man that he needed to change his way of living.

Imagine how ingrained a bad habit is after thirty-eight years. As the gospel story plays out, we see that as soon as the Pharisees put the man on the spot, he deflected the blame for this Sabbath cure onto Jesus. Jesus knew that the man had this tendency and admonished him to be careful. Unfortunately the man once again fell back into the old pattern. He went to the elders and told them that Jesus initiated the cure. The man made sure that he was seen as the victim in that situation.

When a dancer consistently does a step incorrectly, he or she can't blame others. The dancer must learn a whole new way. Likewise, we can break out of the false safety that comes from being a victim. An honest look at our unhealthy patterns of living must be followed by choices that are habitually healthy. We have to learn a new way of living.

Questions for Reflection
• What bad faith habits have I acquired? How can I change my dysfunctional attitudes and actions?

_____

_____

_____

• How do I help others move toward wholeness?

_____

_____

_____

Prayer
Jesus, you were never deterred from your mission. Help me overcome the subtle allure of being the helpless victim, and give me strength to make healthful faith choices.

Wednesday, Fourth Week of Lent

"Can a woman forget her nursing child, or show no compassion for the child of her womb? Even these may forget, yet I will not forget you." **Isaiah 49:15**

Today's reading from Isaiah speaks of an oasis for the soul. As with most oases we come upon this one suddenly. Perhaps we weren't expecting it at all. We have been so caught up in the dance, in the lessons of the desert, that we haven't been watching for the palm trees and cool springs of water. Some of us may feel we don't need this resting-place. We still feel full of energy and enthusiasm and want to keep on moving. Others of us need the rest so badly that we fear this is only a mirage. This place of comfort and refreshment is just too good to be true!

Never, ever, will God forget us! God will not leave us alone to wander endlessly in the desert of loneliness and despair. Never will we be orphaned with no one to hold us in our hours of great sadness. Never will we need to face alone the savage beasts that attack us, regardless of whether they are lurking within our own hearts or prowling in the world around us. God will not abandon us.

Those of us limping through the desert want to submerge ourselves in this love of God. We embrace this loving Mother-God because our journey has revealed to us just how needy we are.

This heart experience is just as important for those of us who are feeling good about our lenten journey. We may be feeling confident right now, but who knows when we'll reach another oasis. There is no shame in needing the loving touch of God, so let us relish the comfort offered today.

Questions for Reflection

• How do I experience God's promise of constant love in my life?

_____

_____

_____

• Am I in need of an oasis of love today? Can I create an oasis in my soul, where Jesus waits for me? What does he want to tell me?

_____

_____

_____

Prayer

You promised, God, that you would never forget me. Sometimes I find that hard to believe, for I seem so small and insignificant. Help me realize that in your eyes I have immeasurable worth.

Thursday, Fourth Week of Lent

"Turn from your fierce wrath; change your mind and do not bring disaster on your people. Remember Abraham, Isaac, and Israel."...And the Lord changed his mind about the disaster that he planned to bring on his people.   **Exodus 32:12–14**

"Where was Moses when the lights went out?" Many of us may recall learning this little rhyme when we were growing up. When we reflect on this lenten reading from Exodus, we might find it helpful to ask the question, "Where was Moses when the lights *were about* to go out?"

An extremely angry God threatened to wipe out the Israelites except for Moses and his descendants. Earlier in this exchange God had even told Moses, "Don't try to stop me." Yet when the lights were about to go out for the Israelites, Moses did not back away, even though he could have. Rather he chose to confront God. He reminded God in no uncertain terms that he had made promises to this group of people.

True relationships are conflicted at times. When two people or a group of people rub shoulders, there are bound to be disagreements and heated words. When people don't have these conflicts, we wonder about the quality of the relationship. We know all this is true with our fellow humans, but do we dare confront God?

Moses didn't mince words or hide his feelings, even though he was talking to God. Their relationship was so solid that Moses didn't fear God's response to confrontation. In fact, God seemed to be pulled up short. How often does God long for us to tell "it" as we see it?

Questions for Reflection

• Do I communicate honestly with God? Does my fear of God inhibit my free expression of frustrations?

_____

_____

_____

• Am I willing to go through conflict to deepen my relationships?

_____

_____

Prayer

Sometimes people don't appreciate honest communication. Because I have felt the sting of their rejection, I have become fearful of speaking my truth. Lord, help me know that it is my honesty you long for in prayer.

Friday, Fourth Week of Lent

"'I have not come on my own. But the one who sent me is true, and you do not know him. I know him, because I am from him, and he sent me.' Then they tried to arrest him." **John 7:28–30**

If you are going to drop a name, it might as well be the big One. We know what it is like when someone brags about knowing a famous person, but what Jesus did was even more remarkable. No doubt the concept of Jesus as the Messiah was a hard sell. He had no credentials for the job. He was the son of a carpenter who came from the dusty little town of Nazareth. He had no special training for this mission, and his message was not what people thought the Messiah should say.

Not only has God sent Jesus, but Jesus declared that he knew God personally. He had to be kidding! No wonder the "good" people of Jerusalem wanted to seize him.

This week we have heard each confrontation Jesus had with the Pharisees, the Sanhedrin, and the people at large. We can feel the build-up of tension in the gospel. Jesus perceived the danger in the situation but did not back down. In fact he seemed to become more emphatic about his mission.

This is the dance of fire, and the heat is building. We know the amount of stamina that is required to move against the grain of common beliefs, as the rhythm becomes staccato. Do we have the strength of faith to endure this kind of crucible? Do I need to confront the status quo around me? Do I hear the One sending me forth?

Questions for Reflection

• What fears keep me silent when I might offer better service by speaking up?

_____

_____

_____

• Who is the Pharisee inside that I need to confront?

_____

_____

_____

Prayer

I pray so often that I not be put to the test yet today, Lord, you invite me to see the importance of standing against the currents of popular sentiment. Give me the courage to foster justice and truth.

Saturday, Fourth Week of Lent

Then the temple police went back to the chief priests and Pharisees, who asked them, "Why did you not arrest him?" The police answered, "Never has anyone spoken like this!"

John 7:45–49

The Pharisees were becoming more comfortable with their role as self-righteous religious leaders. At first they were curious about this Jesus. They even gave the appearance of searching for the truth by engaging Jesus in dialogue. At this point, however, they just wanted to be rid of this man who was making inroads with the ignorant masses. So imagine their frustration when the guards whom they sent out came back empty-handed. "No man ever spoke like that before." These men told the Pharisees that they simply could not arrest someone for speaking the truth, the truth that had obviously stirred their own hearts.

The Pharisees had built their security on their position, their status. They were the chosen because they were educated and held a high rank among the people. They feared that their house of cards might now be crumbling, and Jesus was to blame.

Can Jesus speak through just anybody? As we listen with our hearts to the Spirit who may speak so eloquently through the common person, does fear raise its ugly head? How do we hear the challenges from the wisdom figures we meet in our everyday lives? To hear the words of Jesus in the world today, perhaps we need to let go of our pretenses. We may find the simple truth coming from the person standing right next to us.

Questions for Reflection

• What person or group of people do I think of as lost, not worth bothering about?

• Who has surprised me with their insights? How has my opinion of them changed?

Prayer

Let me hear your wisdom today, Lord, in all who pass my way. May I be humble enough to rejoice in the many different voices singing your song of love.

Fifth Sunday of Lent

He cried with a loud voice, "Lazarus, come out!" The dead man came out, his hands and feet bound with strips of cloth, and his face wrapped in a cloth. Jesus said to them, "Unbind him, and let him go."

John 11:43–44

The main focus of this story is a man called Lazarus. We know that he was a good friend of Jesus but not an apostle. He had two sisters and many, many friends who loved him dearly and grieved his death. We know that Jesus wept for this man and raised him from the dead. Lazarus, for his part, never said a word, and, except for a banquet scene, he never reappeared in the gospel.

Like Lazarus, we have our family and friends, but when we die, comparatively few people will take notice. Like Lazarus some of us might have a moment or two in the sun, but then we return to anonymity.

Fortunately Jesus is the lover of the obscure and ordinary! Just as the death of Lazarus profoundly affects Jesus, so too the pain and suffering, the joys and sorrows of our lives are carried tenderly by our God. In his poem "She Dwelt Among the Untrodden Ways," William Wordsworth writes about a friend who has died, "She lived unknown, and few could know when Lucy ceased to be; but she is in her grave, and, oh, the difference to me!" Jesus says the same to Lazarus and to us. What happens to us makes a difference to Jesus.

Jesus raised Lazarus because he loved him! Certainly Jesus used this incident to teach, and many people came to believe, but as far as Lazarus was concerned there was no other motive than the love of a friend. Jesus wants to take our hand simply because he loves us!

Questions for Reflection

• Who has raised new life in me and expected nothing in return?

_____

_____

_____

• Do I believe that Jesus is head-over-heels in love with me? What difference does this make in my life?

_____

_____

_____

Prayer

What happens in my life makes a difference to you, my God. I do believe, I do believe, I do believe. Amen. Amen. Amen.

Monday, Fifth Week of Lent

Jesus said to her, "Woman, where are they? Has no one condemned you?" She said, "No one, sir." And Jesus said, "Neither do I condemn you. Go your way, and from now on do not sin again." **John 8:9–11**

Humans would like to think that we have advanced since the time of Jesus. Yet women in certain cultures today still run the risk of death by stoning if they commit adultery. In our own country people are still beaten to death because of race, sexual preference, or religious beliefs. We hear these terrible stories and cannot believe them.

As we look at the world around us and shake our heads at these atrocities, perhaps we also need to look at the rock quarries within our own hearts. What are the stones I am fashioning to throw at my neighbor? Who have I condemned with my speech or actions? My jagged little stones may be ever so gently tossed into the path of another, but they have the power to gash feet and cause the person to fall.

When we place ourselves in the position of the adulterous woman rather than the self-righteous, then we stand before God devoid of defenses. We come to know that our sins are not beyond God's forgiveness. Accepting our sin and God's forgiveness enables us to see that we do not need to cast any stones at the person walking along side us.

When we're concentrating on hitting another person with our verbal rocks, it's hard to keep in step with God. When we let God smash these missiles, we find that the remaining grains of sand don't go very far nor do they have much effect on my neighbor.

Questions for Reflection

• What kind of stones do I throw? Who am I to judge others?

_____

_____

_____

• When I have no stones to throw, I'm vulnerable like the woman. Can I live with my vulnerability?

_____

_____

_____

Prayer

I have discovered some rather hefty stones emerging from the soil of my daily living during this lenten journey. Jesus, transform them into soft grains of sand that will not impede the steps of my neighbor.

Tuesday, Fifth Week of Lent

The people spoke against God and against Moses, "Why have you brought us up out of Egypt to die in the wilderness? For there is no food and no water, and we detest this miserable food." **Numbers 21:4–5**

I have an image of the Hebrews wandering in the desert. I see God sitting in the clouds with his eyes closed, yet knowing exactly in what part of the desert his people are located. He knows this because of the constant whine that accompanies them wherever they go. Nag, nag, nag. Nothing was ever right. The people were never satisfied.

How difficult it is for the whiner to dance with the grace of God. Sitting in our misery makes it impossible to find joy in the invitation to dance. Blessings go undetected by those who perpetually complain. If we don't want to end up like the lonely whiner, we pray that God will change our hearts. We pray for a new way of looking at the world around us. While we pray, we begin to make deliberate efforts to find the joy and the blessings of life. Positive living is a choice we make. Instead of complaining about what we don't have in life, we thank God for what we have been given.

All of us have met people we think should be bitter. We look at their lives and say, "They have had so many hard knocks, so much pain." We wonder at the joyful way they live in spite of everything that has befallen them. Perhaps the secret to their ability to live beyond the hardships comes from their gratitude for all the little blessings along the way. Their focus is not so much on what they didn't receive or what was taken from them, as it is upon the presence of God in the midst of it all.

Questions for Reflections

• What is the benefit of whining and saying, "Poor me"? How do I move from being a whiner to being a joyful dancer?

_____

_____

_____

• What blessings in my life can I give thanks for today?

_____

_____

_____

Prayer

I can make a choice to see the good in life or to focus on the difficulties. Lord, change my whining into worship. Let me concentrate on the blessings in life so that the burdens can be shouldered more comfortably.

Wednesday, Fifth Week of Lent

Jesus said to them, "If you were Abraham's children, you would be doing what Abraham did, but now you are trying to kill me, a man who has told you the truth that I heard from God. This is not what Abraham did. You are indeed doing what your father does." **John 8:39–41**

Have you ever had the experience of listening to someone very intently, when suddenly the person throws you a curve, a piece of information you didn't expect to hear? The zinger at the end of

Jesus' quote today reminds me of this kind of experience. Jesus was clearly not speaking of Abraham in his last statement. Since the people were intensely engaged in the argument, they may have needed a couple of seconds to realize what he was saying; but when they did they were furious.

When we are confronted with the truth, it is sometimes a very painful experience. If we are not ready to hear about our failings, then conflict may occur, and who likes to deal with conflict? Truth tellers are willing to face the opposition because the truth is all that matters.

Jesus speaks as the advocate for the poor, the homeless, the mentally ill, the abused, and the unborn child. Jesus speaks the truth through those who will not let us forget that the children of God include everyone. Jesus speaks when our best friend challenges our actions, or our family member insists that we recognize our destructive behavior. We need courage to tell the truth and to hear it. And we need Jesus to help us do both.

Questions for Reflection

• Have I ever had to face conflict in order to confront someone with the truth? Did it make a difference?

_____

_____

_____

• What "truth" might Jesus be asking me to speak to my friend, family member, coworker, government, world?

_____

_____

_____

Prayer

It is a difficult task to confront someone with the truth, and it is just as difficult to hear the words of challenge addressed to me. Help me, Jesus, to honestly hear and speak the truth.

Thursday, Fifth Week of Lent

Jesus said to them, "Very truly, I tell you, before Abraham was, I am." So they picked up stones to throw at him, but Jesus hid himself and went out of the temple.   John 8:56–59

Rocks seemed to be the weapon of choice for the Jews of Jesus' time. They were readily available, and certainly could inflict great injury or death. Jesus wasn't a rock thrower, but he did get his points across by using rocks. In today's reading he points out that he and God are one. For the Jews this was blasphemy and punishable by death, and for an enraged crowd that meant using rocks.

We still find people throwing rocks today, but in places like Jerusalem and Palestine they are now the weapons of the powerless. To throw a rock in anger today could instantly cost your life. Bullets, after all, are more effective than rocks!

What of Jesus' message today? Some still consider it blasphemy, others hear it indifferently, and still others embrace it zealously. How has the Christian family lived out the teaching of Jesus? Is this what Jesus had in mind or would he like to hide himself and slip away once again?

When Jesus points out the big truths of life to me, do I react in anger because it's too much for me to swallow, or do I pause to let my reactionary anger cool and allow the truth to transform my heart?

Questions for Reflection

• Do I find that I react in anger when confronted? Where is Jesus in my response?

_____

_____

_____

• Can I believe that Jesus truly lives in those around me?

_____

_____

_____

Prayer

Jesus, in the depths of my heart I desire to know you, but that means I need to be vulnerable enough to accept your truth in the world around me. May I not become frightened and angry when I find your face revealed in my neighbor.

Friday, Fifth Week of Lent

Many came to Jesus, and they were saying, "John performed no sign, but everything that John said about this man was true." And many believed in him there. John 10:40–42

In the Native American tradition there is a belief that when a person feels overwhelmed by the hassles and turmoil of the world, the person should lie down on the earth and look up at the sky. In doing so the individual once again becomes grounded, once again understands the relationship between themselves and the universe.

Perhaps Jesus understands the wisdom of such actions, for he too returned to the place where it all started for him, the desert. Here Jesus found the followers of John. They came to Jesus with an open mind because John, a man of great integrity, had encouraged them to do so. Many of these people began to believe in Jesus.

Unlike the first time Jesus walked into the desert and found only the temptations of Satan, this time Jesus found community. He found other people who had determined that truth could be found in the desert. Here was a community of faith. Here Jesus could find rest and encouragement. Here he found an oasis.

We cannot walk our faith journey alone. Sharing our lives with others creates a safety net for our shattered dreams and the longings of our heart. Sometimes we seem to be dancing on a tightrope. Isn't it nice to have a net of faithful companions for security?

Questions for Reflection

• Who are the people who believed in me without seeing signs and wonders? Have I thanked them?

_____

_____

_____

• When and where do I go away to reconnect with my spirit, with the universe, and with God?

_____

_____

_____

Prayer

Today, Lord, may I offer you a prayer of thanksgiving for all the companions of faith I have met along the way. You have blessed me with many people who have revealed your face to me, and I am deeply grateful.

Saturday, Fifth Week of Lent

Caiaphas, who was high priest that year, said to them, "You do not understand that it is better for you to have one man die for the people than to have the whole nation destroyed."

John 11:49–50

Have you ever read this part of the gospel and found yourself saying, "Come on, Caiaphas, think about what you are doing!" In fact, it well may be that "thinking" was the one thing Caiaphas did well. He used all his intellectual powers, but did not listen, or observe, or analyze from the heart. Thinking may have been his big mistake.

Heart decisions involve more than the intellect. These choices involve an honest search for the truth, even if that truth defies rational understanding. In this situation Caiaphas was closed off to that kind of searching. He did not go deep enough to experience the Spirit of God speaking. Above all, he feared becoming suspect himself. He believed that the rational thing to do would be to have one man die rather than run the risk of many deaths. That does seem logical, doesn't it?

People of faith are certainly called to be informed and to approach life using their intelligence, but we need to be careful that we don't make our minds the only dance partner. Faith demands that we engage in the dance at deeper places in our heart. Imagine if Jesus used only his intellect and only did what was smart or clever or rational? Faith takes us beyond surface feelings, beyond intelligence, and places us in the realm of mystery. Here we can say, "This may not feel right, this may not seem logical, but I *believe* this is what God wants."

Questions for Reflection

• Have I ever found myself taking a leap in faith? Did it take me beyond reason?

_____

_____

_____

• What is the most foolish but holy thing I've ever done? Was it worth it?

_____

_____

_____

Prayer

Jesus, I realize at times that there is a Caiaphas inside of me that rationalizes poor choices because I am threatened. Help me let go of control long enough to make room for your mysterious revelations of faith.

Passion Sunday

"I gave my back to those who struck me, and my cheeks to those who pulled out the beard. The Lord God helps me; therefore I have set my face like flint, and I know that I shall not be put to shame."   **Isaiah 50:4–7**

How could Jesus ride into Jerusalem amid the waving palms and shouting crowds, knowing what would be in store for him? Isaiah gives us important clues today. Jesus, the suffering servant, was in communication each and every day with his Father. Throughout his life Jesus was faithful to this relationship, and daily he practiced the steps of surrender. When this last week came, he was ready to set his face like flint and embrace this demanding dance partner. If that meant leaving the light of day to lean into the shadows, then so be it. For Jesus doing his Father's will had become as natural as breathing.

Jesus knew that living in the presence of truth would never lead to disgrace. Suffering, pain, and human ridicule could all be endured because his source of strength was always present.

How often are we afraid to speak out or to act with Christian charity because we are concerned about what people will think or about how we will be perceived? During this whole lenten journey we have seen Jesus function with little regard for worldly perceptions. On this triumphant Sunday, while others around him perceived this entrance as a great victory, Jesus saw it for what it was, the last rally before the end, the first movement in a deadly dance. Beyond the wildest imaginings of those present that Palm Sunday, Jesus saw so much more!

Questions for Reflection

• On this first day of Holy Week, do I find myself lost in the desert or hand-in-hand with Jesus on the road to Jerusalem? Can I make an all-out effort to practice the will of God this week?

_____

_____

_____

• What can I do this week to respond to the needs of my neighbor?

_____

_____

_____

Prayer

Lord, when I see that following you will lead to suffering I become sick at heart. On this Passion Sunday, give me the courage to shoulder the crosses of life that will glorify you.

Monday of Holy Week

Mary took a pound of costly perfume made of pure nard, anointed Jesus' feet, and wiped them with her hair. The house was filled with the fragrance of the perfume. **John 12:3**

Jesus was having dinner at the home of Lazarus, Martha, and Mary. Lazarus was present but silent at this banquet. Martha was serving a meal again. And Mary, well, Mary was being Mary. Dramatically she knelt and poured very expensive perfume over Jesus' feet. In front of everyone she dried his feet with her hair. The whole house was filled with the aroma. To the surprise of some of the guests Jesus approved of her actions.

Artists know that in order to capture an audience, they have to engage the senses. They also know that to the practical-minded person, art often seems to be a waste of time and energy. Reading poetry, walking through an art gallery, listening to music accomplishes nothing in the practical world, does it? Ah, but what a wonderful waste of time it is! It feeds the soul and lightens our step. Listening to good music, for example, can soothe the weary spirit and can keep us in touch with our deepest emotions.

Mary's actions were her artistic expression of love. They were her way of saying what words would have been inadequate to convey. Mary's work of art was created from the heart. Like any masterpiece, her art remains timeless.

Questions for Reflection
• Is my life too practical? What energizing thing could I do today?

_____

_____

_____

- Jesus saw the symbolism of the anointing in relationship to his burial. Has God ever spoken symbolically to me? How?

_____

_____

_____

Prayer

In my practical living out of Christian values I sometimes forget that there is an artist inside of me. Jesus, help me find creative ways to express the beauty of your love.

Tuesday of Holy Week

Peter said to him, "Lord, why can I not follow you now? I will lay down my life for you." Jesus answered, "Very truly, I tell you, before the cock crows, you will have denied me three times." **John 13:36–38**

When I was a teenager I thought that if anyone ever tried to rob me, I would fight. I wouldn't allow anyone to take my possessions! Yet when I was the unfortunate victim of a mugging, in my mid-twenties, I did absolutely nothing to impede the robber.

In our gospel Peter was pretty full of himself, wasn't he? After all, he was the rock. The church was going to be built on him, wasn't it? In grandiose fashion he proclaimed that he would lay down his life for Jesus. "Nothing to it" he seemed to say. At this point in the gospel there was a real gap between Peter the fisherman and the man who would one day be called Saint Peter. While Jesus was on his journey toward Calvary, Peter was on an ego trip. While

Jesus knew exactly what he was talking about, Peter didn't have any idea what he was saying.

Peter wasn't aware of what he would do when faced with an overwhelming fear for his own life. Peter was about to fall. He was about to learn that his courage would not come from machismo but from anchoring himself to Jesus, the source of his real strength and courage. His dependency on God was not yet strong enough, but he would get there. Eventually Peter would learn that when faith is strong, we don't need to brag about what we will do; we simply do it.

Questions for Reflection

• Have I ever found myself making statements I regret later? How did that feel?

_____

_____

_____

• How sure am I of my faith? What have I built in on?

_____

_____

_____

Prayer

Lord, when I am faced with the possibility of suffering, my knees buckle and at times I slink off in fear. May I take heart when I read this gospel because a failure in practice does not have to be the end of the story.

Wednesday of Holy Week

Jesus answered, "Woe to that one by whom the Son of Man is betrayed!"...Judas, who betrayed him, said, "Surely not I, Rabbi?" He replied, "You have said so." **Matthew 26:23–25**

"I'm never going to dance again. Guilty feet have got no rhythm. Should have known better than to cheat a friend and waste the chance that I'd been given." These words from George Michael's song, *Careless Whisper*, seem appropriate for Judas, the fallen apostle. After living shoulder to shoulder with Jesus for three years, Judas was never quite able to follow the dance.

Judas and Peter both betrayed Jesus in the final days. Whereas Peter's denial was spoken out of fear and anguish, Judas' sin was premeditated, calculated, and cunning. Judas always seemed to be balancing the pros and cons, the advantages and disadvantages, the risks and benefits. Judas liked sitting on the fence and watching which way the wind blew. He wanted power, and he thought he could manipulate Jesus to achieve it. For Judas the bottom line was, "What's in it for me?"

Judas finally sank into a hole of pain and despair. All his planning, all his scheming blew up in his face and the worst part was that people knew whom to blame. He could not face that humiliation.

Judas' lesson is powerful. When we betray the trust of the person closest to our heart, we lose our way; we become like a ship without a rudder. When we control a situation to our advantage, we need to ask ourselves, "Where is God in this planning?"

Questions for Reflection

• Have I ever betrayed someone's trust? How did I feel? What did I learn?

_____

_____

• What is the most difficult thing about trying to reestablish trust?

_____

_____

_____

Prayer

Christ Jesus, keep me honest in our relationship. Make me realize my small decisions are self-serving, for I never want to reach a point where I might choose myself over you in the more important decisions of life.

Holy Thursday

"If I, your Lord and Teacher, have washed your feet, you also ought to wash one another's feet. For I have set you an example, that you also should do as I have done to you." John 13:12–15

As the old woman shuffled along the sidewalk, she complained to her companion, "When your feet hurt, you hurt all over! You can't stand; you can't walk, and you can't think about anything else but finding a place to sit down." Perhaps Jesus had a sense of what that kind of discomfort was like.

When we are cleaned and refreshed, we can put our best foot forward in life. In symbolic fashion Jesus offered this gift to his disciples. Once he convinced them to let him minister to them, he challenged them to do the same for the people they would meet along the way. He asked them to see that giving people a fresh start through compassionate love was the most important service they could render.

How many of us want to get down to the level of our neighbor's feet? How many of us can acknowledge that we need someone else's help to refresh ourselves? As we hold the foot of our neighbor to our heart, can we embrace the arches of support that bind us together and kiss the calloused heels of hope that buffer us through all the traumas of life? In the sacred action of washing can we consecrate the feet of our neighbor to the service of the Dancer?

Questions for Reflection

• Has anyone washed the soles of my soul lately? How did it feel?

_____

_____

_____

• Have I ever offered to wash the sacred soul of my neighbor? Did they appreciate it or reject it?

_____

_____

_____

Prayer

My feet are dragging today, Lord, but my neighbors can't even walk. Help me to wash away their pain and lighten their step. May they come to know you through my words and actions.

Good Friday

But he was wounded for our transgressions, crushed for our iniquities; upon him was the punishment that made us whole, and by his bruises we are healed.   **Isaiah 53:5**

The Backstreet Boys sing in a hit song, "Show me the meaning of being lonely." Some situations in life lead us into loneliness, and we need to be able to embrace those not-so-pleasant moments. Sometimes, in order to deepen our trust in God, we need to experience abandonment, the sense that God is missing from our hearts. It is not an easy place to dwell. It is the starkest part of the desert.

Dancing to Calvary is not for the faint-hearted. Physical pain, ridicule, and rejection are all painful dance partners, but when the beacon of love that has sustained us through the whole journey seems to have gone out, the journey is much more difficult. In this moment of abandonment Jesus made the ultimate leap of faith and kept his eyes focused on the will of God. He did not struggle against it or try to escape it. According to the old Shaker hymn, *Lord of the Dance*, Jesus "danced on a Friday when the sky turned black. It's hard to dance with the devil on your back." Indeed, it was almost impossible for Jesus, but because he was able to dance up that hill, we know salvation today. Jesus, the forsaken one, was willing to carry our infirmities upon his shoulders.

Can we understand the fact that Jesus is willing to die for us again today? For our sins, our failings, for our redemption the Lamb is willing to lay down his life. If all the people on the planet disappeared and the "we" became only "me," do I know in my heart that he would still embrace the cross and die?

Questions for Reflection

• Do I understand that loneliness is essential to growing in faith?

_____

_____

_____

• What is my greatest failing? Can I lay it on Jesus' back?

_____

_____

_____

Prayer

I really cannot comprehend that you, the Son of God, would die for my soul, but I do believe that you would. In the times when my belief is shaken to the core, may my eyes remain fixed on you.

Holy Saturday

In the garden there was a new tomb in which no one had ever been laid. And so, because it was the Jewish day of Preparation, and the tomb was nearby, they laid Jesus there.   John 19: 41–42

It is quiet around the gravesite. In the lives of those of us who saw Jesus as the Messiah, everything has come to a crashing halt. After the frenzied activities of the trial and the climax of death upon a tree, the world is quiet. Birds sing, insects buzz, and the winds still blow, but in the hollowed out spaces of our hearts all is quiet. Everything has been poured out from our spirits in this final dance of death.

Yet quiet is good. After the last dance on Calvary, we need the quiet, we need the silence. We can hear what we could not hear with all the blaring music. In a desert that seems to go on forever, we come to a stop. Today we look back at all the dancing we have done these past forty days. We have had some fine times, haven't we? We have seen what we have never seen before, heard what can only be called "the truth," and we have learned to step gracefully into life and death. But now that it's over, was it really worth it?

How long have we been here now? Six hours, twelve hours, twenty-four, thirty-six? How does one keep track of time in this void? Let it go! It is finished. So what are we waiting for? It's a little foolish trying to hear music in the cave of death, but perhaps a part of us is doing just that. How can we ever expect to pick up a beat buried in this grief and pain? Forget it, forget him! Not yet? Let's wait a little while longer? Wait...do I hear what I think I hear?

Questions for Reflection

• How do I observe this day? How quiet is my soul today?

_____

_____

_____

• What graces have I received this Lent? Has my desert dancing been insightful for me? Have I grown in my love of Jesus?

_____

_____

— _____

Prayer

Without the complete and utter silence of this Holy Saturday, I would be unable to pick up the first tiny sounds of the resurrection. Jesus, help me quiet my mind today so I might discover the joy of your resurrection.

Easter Sunday

The angel said to the women, "Do not be afraid; I know that you are looking for Jesus who was crucified. He is not here; for he has been raised, as he said." Suddenly Jesus met them and said, "Greetings!" And they came to him, took hold of his feet, and worshiped him.   **Matthew 28:5–6, 9**

What a day this is, what a wonderful, wonderful day! Today new life begins. Jesus is risen today. Salvation is at hand. So dance, my friends, dance on the table, dance in the field. Dance because you can't do anything else. Dance with Mary Magdalene and the other Mary as they race from the tomb to spread the word. Never has a word wanted to be spread as this one does.

Look! Who is standing here in front of you now? You said good-bye to him so painfully on the shores of your dreams. Hope seemed to sail away on a cross of death, but now feast your eyes on the love of your life. He is beautiful, and now so are you. You are bathed in this Easter light. You have not left the desert behind, but oh, has it changed. He greets you and sends you to tell the good news that he will see everyone in Galilee. Now you are running, jumping and, yes, you're dancing again. The dance is recklessly uninhibited, and isn't it fun!

Today you may be confined to bed in a nursing home; you may be wheeling your chair down the street; you may be sitting in a prison; or you may be hiding those Easter eggs for the kids, but inside your heart this day, you are sprinting with those Marys. You know what it feels like, yet you are unable to describe it. He is risen in your heart. Alleluia, alleluia! Spread the news far and wide. Jesus lives. He is not dead. And if your heart is so tangled in joy that you don't know what to do…dance, dance, dance!!!

Questions for Reflection

• Easter is about being in the presence of God and experiencing joy, so forget the questions today. Live the answer!

_____

_____

_____

Prayer

Dance in my heart, God of the Living. May I live this dance of Easter joy so that all may catch a glimpse of the Risen Lord.

Monday of Easter Week

The women left the tomb and ran to tell his disciples. Suddenly Jesus met them and said, "Greetings!" Then he said, "Do not be afraid; go and tell my brothers to go to Galilee; there they will see me." **Matthew 28:8–10**

Have you ever watched a child dancing with the waves of the ocean? They creep down the sand toward the water, giggling until the waves start coming at them. Then they dash back up the beach, screeching in fear that the water might catch them. Mary Magdalene and the other Mary must have felt divided between giddiness and fright. Then Jesus greeted them; they must have jumped and screamed as if they had seen a ghost! Immediately Jesus calmed them and told them, "Go and tell my brothers to go to Galilee; there they will see me." No sooner did they recognize him than he sent them off to proclaim the Good News.

The early Christians—and all of us who have followed—did not have to wait until they knew all the deepest truths of their faith before they could act in Jesus' name. There are no prerequisites or degrees needed to be a Christian. To answer our calling as Christians we only need to believe in Jesus and spread the Good News.

Christianity is measured by growth, not perfection. All the small steps we learn along the way make us powerful messengers of truth and love. Eventually if we stay the course, we find that all the elaborate backdrops and themes of the Christian life are variations of call and response. Like the little child dancing with the waves of an ocean, or Mary Magdalene and the other Mary, we may feel both joyful and fearful when Jesus reveals himself to us.

Questions for Reflection

• Have I ever hovered between joy and fear? What was it like?

_____

_____

_____

• When have I been called by God to be his messenger of joy? How did I respond?

_____

_____

_____

Prayer

Risen Lord, I am both excited and frightened when I realize that you are dancing into my life in a new way. May the exciting joy in my heart overcome any fear that would inhibit me from answering your call to service.

Tuesday of Easter Week

Jesus said to her, "Do not hold on to me, because I have not yet ascended to the Father. But go to my brothers and say to them, 'I am ascending to my Father and your Father, to my God and your God.'" **John 20:17**

Mary wanted to freeze time, to hold tight and cling to Jesus. Jesus did not allow her to do so. If she had, he would not have been able to ascend to the Father nor would the Spirit descend upon her and the disciples at Pentecost.

How often are we like Mary, holding on or clinging to people, places, or situations? We don't want things to change because it is hard to adjust. Yet Pentecost, the giving of the Spirit, cannot happen if we are stuck in one place, especially if the place we are stuck in is the past.

What facets of our life do we need to let go of so the new Spirit can come? Is it a grief we've held onto for too long? Maybe we must let go of our long held belief about another person in order to see how that person has grown. Maybe we need to let go of a dream of our youth so the new dream God offers us today can receive its Spirit. Maybe we need to let old hurts rest in the hands of the ascending Christ, so they might be transformed into new energy and vision.

Jesus tells us that the way we were is not the way we are now. Furthermore, who we are today is not who we will be in the future. During this season of Easter look into your heart to find those people, situations, or memories to which you are clinging. Ask Christ to help you let them go. Then prepare for the Pentecost God will offer.

Questions for Reflection
• What memory am I clinging to that impedes the Spirit?

_____

_____

_____

• What event or situation in my life that I haven't accepted has stalled my heart?

_____

_____

_____

Prayer
The past is all I know, Lord, but today you offer me a future filled with joy. Give me the courage to let go of the familiar parts of my life that hold me prisoner in the tomb. Raise me up to new life in you.

Wednesday of Easter Week

Peter said, "I have no silver or gold, but what I have I give you; in the name of Jesus Christ of Nazareth, stand up and walk." And he took him by the right hand and raised him up; and immediately his feet and ankles were made strong.

Acts 3:6–7

After all this time we still haven't figured out that money and worldly power cannot bring happiness. All a person has to do is sit back and watch leaders of powerful countries to see that too often manipulation for gain underlies most political games. Yet if we look into our own hearts, we see that we too are victims of our need to find happiness by accumulating our own kind of silver and gold.

The lame man in the first reading was also seeking money. A few coins tossed his way every day allowed him to survive a while longer. He didn't realize that something greater could be his for the asking. Peter's gift to this man was unexpected and freely given. It was power itself, a power that comes from the Spirit and transforms life.

Look at the wonderful people around us who do not give us silver or gold, but who have given us powerful treasures that have deepened our faith lives. Look at the beauty around us that feeds our souls at no charge. Look at those who give us the gift of hope we didn't even know we were starving for, or the gift of love we didn't think could be ours to cherish. Relationships are free to those who will accept them. The air is free to those who would breathe. I can dance anywhere, at anytime, and the ability to express myself is free. I can offer the presence of God to my neighbor, and that is free as well.

Questions for Reflection

• Who has given me more than what I thought I needed?

_____

_____

_____

• What could I offer to someone today that would be better than silver or gold?

_____

_____

_____

Prayer

Your gift of faith, Lord, received at my baptism, gives me limitless resources to call upon in my need. Your love, Lord, is all I will ever desire. Help me remember today how very blessed I am.

Thursday of Easter Week

"Why are you frightened, and why do doubts arise in your hearts? Look at my hands and my feet; see that it is I myself. Touch me and see; for a ghost does not have flesh and bones as you see that I have."
                                                                    Luke 24:38–39

Two of the disciples told the other disciples a fantastic story about their encounter with Jesus. The active imaginations of the others naturally led them to believe that the two disciples must have seen a ghost. Like fearful wide-eyed children, they marveled at the tale.

Suddenly, Jesus appeared. While the hearts of the disciples pounded with adrenaline, Jesus asked them, "Why are you frightened?" We cannot help but think that Jesus was having a little fun with his friends. Yet what more gentle way was there to defuse the anxiety and worry than by asking questions that made the disciples think and look beyond their experience of terror? Jesus then asked them to give him something to eat, to function at some level. By eating food he showed them very clearly that he was flesh and blood.

Sometimes life is overwhelming. When we cannot comprehend all the choices and chaos around us, we become fearful and start to panic. At those times we need to look for the person of Jesus to appear in our midst. We need to listen to the questions he will ask us, questions that can bring a sense of reality to our troubled souls.

Jesus asks us to look inside ourselves to find out why we feel frightened. He asks us to move beyond our fear and step toward the acceptance of joy. If we do so, we may discover that there is reality in front of us more amazing than any ghost could be.

Questions for Reflection

• What question could Jesus ask me that would astound me?

_____

_____

_____

• How much proof do I require of God in order to believe?

_____

_____

_____

Prayer

Jesus, in those moments when you wish to reveal yourself to me, may my fright not block my openness to your presence. Help me know that you are as real as the air I breathe and not a figment of my imagination.

Friday of Easter Week

Jesus said to them, "Cast the net to the right side of the boat, and you will find some (fish)." So they cast it, and now they were not able to haul it in because there were so many fish.

John 21:5–6

A grandfather loved to take his grandson out on Saturday afternoon trips to the lake. They could just throw their line in and watch to see if the fish would grab the bait. Once the grandfather said, "Just remember, when you're worried about something, you can always go fishing." The boy replied, "Why would I want to do that,

Grandpa?" The grandfather said, "While you are sitting there relaxing, enjoying nature, and waiting for the big one to bite, sometimes a solution to your problem just kind of pops up all on its own."

Perhaps the apostles in the boat were thinking along the same lines. For three years they had lived and worked with Jesus. They loved him and were deeply grieved when he was crucified. Then the disciples had to deal with the revelation that Jesus was alive. Maybe while they fished, they could make some sense of all that had transpired. But after fishing all night and catching nothing, they still had no answers. Suddenly Jesus called out to them and asked if they had caught anything. When they told him they hadn't, he suggested they try on the right side. All at once, they had so many fish they didn't know what to do with them.

There was something playful in the resurrected Jesus. We often forget that God invented fun and likes to engage in it once in a while. In the end, because these men took the time to go fishing, the answer to their questions and their concerns appeared right before them. Their joy was as abundant as their catch.

Questions for Reflection

• How do I relax so I can hear the word of God more clearly?

_____

_____

_____

• Does my God have a sense of humor?

_____

_____

_____

Prayer

Lord, help me let go, relax, and just have fun with you. Teach me that sometimes the important questions of life become clearer when I engage my mind and body in a familiar routine.

Saturday of Easter Week

When they saw the boldness of Peter and John and realized that they were uneducated and ordinary men, they were amazed and recognized them as companions of Jesus.

Acts 4:13–15

Don't the rulers, elders, and scribes in this Scripture passage seem rather familiar? Perhaps the faces are different, maybe the names have changed, but the attitude closely resembles that of the Pharisees and scribes who found Jesus all too much. In this episode they could not understand how anything of consequence could have taken place because, after all, Peter and John were uneducated and ordinary. The leaders were cautious because they didn't want to upset the people, so they didn't say anything publicly. However, it was obvious they would rather be rid of this ignorant rabble than deal with them.

Peter and John, on the other hand, do not seem like the apostles of Christ found in the gospels, do they? In fact they were the same people, they had the same names but the Spirit that lived in them was very different. Now they were courageous and proactive, happy to find their power in solidarity with the poor.

Most of us fit the category of ordinary people, and while the common person may have more education than in the past, many of us still don't have theological degrees. Yet in the ordinary person the Spirit is alive and well. The heart of the believer is the essential thing, not the education. The eyes of those grounded in their faith have a clear vision, not the eyes of those who sit on the lofty seats of self-righteousness.

Questions for Reflection

• What in my own life indicates that the Spirit is alive and well?

_____

_____

_____

• Do I ever judge someone who does not have the same education or status as I do?

_____

_____

_____

Prayer

Holy Spirit, you filled the apostles with wisdom, understanding, courage, and power. You gave simple men extraordinary gifts. Help me know that regardless of my status in life, these gifts are given to me as well.

Second Sunday of Easter

"Although you have not seen him, you love him; and even though you do not see him now, you believe in him and rejoice with an indescribable and glorious joy, for you are receiving the outcome of your faith." **Peter 1:8–9**

The stance toward God that we call faith is pure gift to us. We did not earn it. We cannot give faith away to someone else, even though we may desire that they have the gift. Sometimes we experience great sorrow because those we love don't seem to have the gift of faith or they don't seem to be excited about their relationship with God. But because we are people of faith we believe God is working in their lives in ways that we may not be able to fathom.

In faith, Peter tells us, we are blessed because we love what we cannot see. We have never seen the person of Jesus yet we love him. That is incredible isn't it? Many would say it is foolish. How can people put their lives on the line for a God they have never seen? For the unbeliever it is crazy, but for those who have faith, all things are possible.

Faith is not a static but a dynamic dance. It grows deeper as we find signs of God's presence. Faithful eyes see God in the world of nature. True believers hear God in the words of Scripture or the cries of a newborn child. Pilgrim people find the risen Savior manifested in the unexpected heroes and heroines in our midst, those who lay down their lives for their less fortunate neighbors. God touches the beloved disciple in the quiet, private moments of prayer, when the living presence of Jesus offers insights, wisdom, and consolation.

As people of faith we don't need to touch the side of Jesus to know that he lives, because *he* has touched us.

Questions for Reflection

• How often do I offer a prayer of thanksgiving for the gift of faith?

_____

_____

_____

• Can I recall a time when God changed me forever?

_____

_____

_____

Prayer

Christ Jesus, may I always cherish your gift of faith and never take it for granted. May I continue to find your presence in all of creation and in every circumstance of life.

Second Monday of Easter

Nicodemus said to him, "How can anyone be born after having grown old?" Jesus answered, "Very truly, I tell you, no one can enter the kingdom of God without being born of water and Spirit."

John 3:4–6

Fearful that someone would see him, Nicodemus met with Jesus in the middle of the night. Nicodemus, a leading member of the Sanhedrin and a learned man, sought understanding from an itinerant preacher but only under the cover of darkness. How can anyone be born after having grown old? How many of us look at Nicodemus and find ourselves saying, "What a dumb question to ask!" Of course everyone knows that Jesus isn't talking about a physical rebirth but a birth in the Holy Spirit.

Perhaps poor Nicodemus is more like us than we would like to imagine. Nicodemus was afraid to talk with Jesus in the daylight, yet was urged by the Spirit to seek the truth. Nicodemus, a good and decent man, tried to dance on the tightrope stretched between the righteous orthodoxy of his religion and the compelling pull of the message Jesus was proclaiming. I believe in Jesus but perhaps find it uncomfortable to speak about my faith openly. I find myself asking God some pretty stupid questions at times too. I ask, "Who are you going to send to help the poor?" when I should be looking in the mirror.

We can be like the questioning Nicodemus as long as we also try to be like the courageous Nicodemus who anointed the body of Jesus at the burial. In the moment of truth we can be like Nicodemus and minister without having all the answers.

Questions for Reflection

• What question do I ask Jesus more than any other? Could asking the question from a different angle help me hear God's response?

_____

_____

_____

• Why am I afraid to share my faith with the people around me?

_____

_____

Prayer

Lord, I want to follow, but I am afraid to step out into the world around me to proclaim my beliefs. When you call me to move beyond the darkness, may I respond courageously in the light of day.

Second Tuesday of Easter

The wind blows where it chooses, and you hear the sound of it, but you do not know where it comes from or where it goes. So it is with everyone who is born of the Spirit. John 3:8

In the 1960s the singing trio of Peter, Paul, and Mary popularized a Bob Dylan song entitled, _Blowin' in the Wind_. The song questioned how long people would try to solve their problems through war and violence. The answer to all the questions the song posed is the same: "The answer is blowin' in the wind." In our world today we are still asking the same questions because we still rely on the old ways of solving our differences. Thus, the answers are still blowing in the wind. They are blowing in the wind of the Spirit who desperately seeks space in our hearts.

The Spirit who moves where he pleases can come from a direction we least expect. The Spirit can touch someone we never thought could become a spokesperson for peace. The Spirit of Peace is not found in the winds of war but in the gentle, almost unnoticed breeze that can be the beginning of a mighty stimulus for good.

In order for this Spirit to have free reign in our world, we must be open to mystery, to surprise, to a new wind. Isn't that what Easter is all about—believing in new life and new realities? During this Easter season become aware of which way the wind of the Spirit is blowing by going deep into your heart and claiming the truth of that Spirit. Don't worry about why the Spirit is moving within or where it wants to take you. Just allow yourself to blow with the wind. The answers will follow.

Questions for Reflection

• After praying to the Spirit, can I list at least five creative ways to deal with a conflict I am now facing in my life? Can I try one?

_____

_____

_____

• How could I organize people to be a force for mass construction?

_____

_____

_____

Prayer

There is a fresh wind blowing in my heart. It is the Spirit of resurrection that offers me a new perspective on life. May I always celebrate the winds of change that you initiate in my life and in my world.

Second Wednesday of Easter

Then someone arrived and announced, "Look, the men whom you put in prison are standing in the temple and teaching the people!" Then the captain went with the temple police and brought them, but without violence, for they were afraid of being stoned by the people. **Acts 5:25–26**

The world revolves around opinion polls. We may think this poll-taking is a relatively new phenomenon, but consumer sentiment was tracked even in the time of Christ. The difference is that the poll results two thousand years ago were very pointed and called for an immediate adjustment to the will of the crowd. In an angry crowd of citizens one probably did not take time to write down the percentage of the unfavorable rating because you may have been busy running for your life. A crowd with stones tended to get an immediate reaction.

If we are sensitive to the numerous occasions when stonings are mentioned in the New Testament, we will notice a shift. In the gospel Jesus encountered angry crowds with stones on several different occasions, while in the first part of the Acts of Apostles it is the organized religious leaders who were fearful of the crowds. Perhaps over time truth-telling wears down the arguments of the opposition. Eventually truth will win out, and opinion will shift toward genuine life.

Jesus died for the truth, but his truth had a life of its own, a life that rose to new and more powerful life in the apostles after Pentecost. So rejoice, for slowly, the truth will shed light, and the courage of truth tellers will hold sway in the world.

Questions for Reflection

• In which group of people am I afraid to tell the truth?

_____

_____

_____

• Do I back down from a situation because I am afraid of what people will say, or because I want to disguise my motives?

_____

_____

_____

Prayer

My God, this world seems to be in such a mess. Many of us find it so difficult to hold on to hope amid the death and destruction that surround us. Give us eyes to see that even in chaos your kingdom is being established.

Second Thursday of Easter

"'We gave you strict orders not to teach in this name, yet here you have filled Jerusalem with your teaching.' But Peter and the apostles answered, 'We must obey God rather than any human authority.'"   **Acts 5:28–29**

The leaders of the Sanhedrin scolded the apostles as a parent scolds a child for misbehaving, but the truth is that the local spiritual leaders were not aligned with the will of the Father. Imagine how steamed the Sanhedrin was because the apostles ignored their dictates, and the people embraced this man called Jesus. Futhermore they were furious that they were being held accountable for his death. As they realized they were beginning to lose control, they tried to find grounds on which to assert their authority, but the ground was crumbling beneath their feet.

Yet these types of people cannot keep the Word of God from spreading throughout the world! Of course, there will be times when we will be puzzled by the events that take place around us. We may grieve that we have missed opportunities to spread the Word. We may anguish over the seeming victories of evil, but deep down we need to know that the mission of Christ cannot be stopped.

The Easter season celebrates power. Beyond our realm of understanding there is wonderful news that death has been overcome by the resurrection, and that makes Christians extremely powerful.

So let all the little sputtering steam pots around us sound off. Let those who are affronted by the truth be affronted. Let those who treasure security and position more than honesty and love have their day. In the end it will not matter, for truth will win the day, and grace will spill over into the world around us. Let's rejoice in the victory that is assured for all disciples of the truth.

Questions for Reflection

• What truth has been set free in me this Easter season?

_____

_____

_____

• Is there something I treasure more than truth?

_____

_____

_____

Prayer

The victory is yours, Lord. Alleluia. The victory is ours as well. The powers of this world cannot hold me if I live in you, Jesus. Alleluia, Amen.

Second Friday of Easter

Gamaliel, a teacher of the law, respected by all the people said, "If this plan or this undertaking is of human origin, it will fail; but if it is of God, you will not be able to overthrow them."

Acts 5:34, 38–39

If you have ever been to a state or federal park, you will often find a naturalist on staff. This person's job is to study the flora and fauna of the park and make decisions about the ongoing maintenance of the ecosystems in that area. The naturalist who spends time observing can become the wise expert who helps unlock the mysteries of nature for the common person.

Something about a wise person commands respect from those around. He or she is often the one who has taken time to sit back and observe before commenting. Wise persons have an ability to hone in on important aspects of a situation and state their case in a clear and concise way. Wise people do not tend to speak in authoritarian ways, but when they speak, their words ring with true authority. Gamaliel seems to have been such a person. While everyone else was at loose ends concerning appropriate ways of dealing with the disciples, Gamaliel simply said, the proof is in the pudding! Be patient, wait it out, see which way the wind blows, let the dust settle before judging these men or this Jesus. Gamaliel suggests that we be like the observant naturalist and track the power of the name of Jesus in the world around us.

In the Shaker hymn *The Lord of the Dance,* the following line can be found: "They buried my body and they thought I'd gone, but I am the dance and I still go on." It suggests that the power of the resurrection lives on. This is a good time to reflect on our past season in order to pick out the patterns that suggest a heavenly future.

Welcoming the Desert

In this desert you will learn the dance of salvation.

Filling the Jar

Barren places hold no fear
for those who possess Living Water.

Draw On Strength from Within

Is your eye on the heart of love?

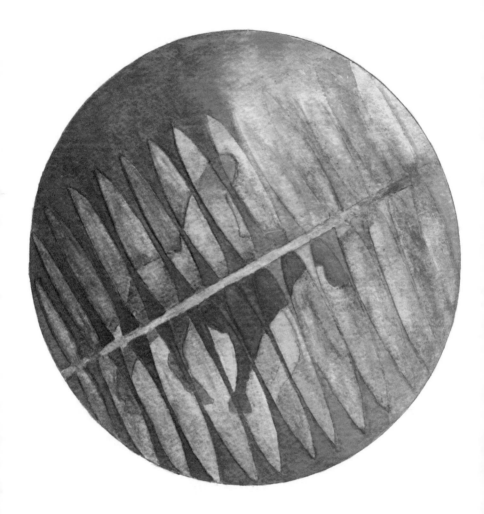

Palm Sunday

"Stand up and raise your heads,
because your redemption is drawing near." *Luke 21:28*

The Persimmon Tree

In Jesus, death opens up a lot of possibilities.

Joy

The Risen Jesus brings joy into our day.

Vulnerable

If God desires that we bloom
then, no matter what, we will!

Harmony Unity in Diversity

The passionate flames of the Spirit
illuminate the language of love.

Questions for Reflection

• What wisdom lessons have I learned by observing life around me?

_____

_____

_____

• Where does the power in my life come from?

_____

_____

_____

Prayer

Spirit of Wisdom, help me become aware of the wisdom figures you have placed in my life. May I be open to the lesson they can teach me.

Second Saturday of Easter

"The one who believes in me will also do the works that I do and, in fact, will do greater works than these. I will do whatever you ask in my name, so that the Father may be glorified in the Son."   **John 14:12–13**

A little lady frequently went to the casino. She put her quarter into the slot machine, pushed the start button, and she said aloud, "In the name of the Lord Jesus Christ give me the jackpot." To the amazement of everyone around her, she won! None of us believe this is what Jesus had in mind when he suggested that we pray in his name. Yet when we concentrate on the second line of this

Scripture quote and ignore the first line, perhaps we, too, think that simply invoking Jesus' name will work like magic.

The key to the credibility of the second line of this passage is that we believe in Jesus enough to do the hard work that he refers to in the first sentence. First of all, there was the work of intense communication, the prayer that he kept up with his Father. Then he stripped away everything that was not essential from his life in order to know what was important and what was not. Next he had the task of becoming compassionate, of learning the desires and hopes of those around him. Finally, he took on the work of self-sacrifice, doing good for others.

If we take these inner tasks seriously, then we too will work marvels beyond our imagining. The work we do will focus attention on the greater glory of God. Our hearts will focus on the deepest needs we can serve. Once we are engaged in all this work, then when we use the name of the Lord Jesus in supplication, we will not be surprised by the results.

Questions for Reflection

• How is my inner work coming along?

_____

_____

_____

• What grace might I ask for to help me in this work?

_____

_____

_____

Prayer

When I pray, may I always remember to put God's will before my own. May I build relationships with my neighbors in such a way that I put their welfare before my own. I ask this in the name of Jesus Christ.

Third Sunday of Easter

When Jesus was at the table with them, he took bread, blessed and broke it, and gave it to them. Then their eyes were opened, and they recognized him....They said to each other, "Were not our hearts burning within us while he was talking to us on the road?"

Luke 24: 29–32

Like the disciples on the road to Emmaus, too often we need something more tangible to help us believe God is present. A burning heart just doesn't seem to be enough. The disciples too needed something more to recognize the presence of Jesus. Once they experienced the breaking of the bread as only Jesus had done it, then they could believe. What is revealed in the meal to these two would transform their lives, would energize them, and would make prophets of them.

They also learned that if they had listened to their burning hearts, they would have known Jesus. We can be sure they would not forget the experience, or what it felt like to have their hearts burning with the presence of God. They would listen more carefully the next time. Even in this moment Jesus was teaching them how to find him.

When we experience the presence of God, how do we know it is God? We all have signposts along our journey of life that point to Jesus' presence. Like the disciples there will be times when we only realize it was God's initiative after the fact. We need not be discouraged if we feel we have been slow in figuring out God's message because God is infinitely patient with the true seeker. He will come again into our midst. In the meantime we can learn how to listen to our hearts.

Questions for Reflection

• How am I able to understand a burning heart in relationship to God?

_____

_____

_____

• What subtle movements of God have I already seen in my life? When I
miss the movement of God, do I become discouraged?

_____

_____

_____

Prayer

*You grace me with your touch, Lord, but I do not always realize that it is
you. Grant that I might be more sensitive to your movement. May I know
that my burning heart is a sign of your presence.*

Third Monday of Easter

"You are looking for me…because you ate your fill of the
loaves. Do not work for the food that perishes, but for the food
that endures for eternal life, which the Son of Man will give
you." **John 6:26–27**

Have you ever been on a committee, a board of directors, or
belonged to an organization that had a meal coinciding with the
meeting? Let's face it, if we have to go to a boring meeting, at least
some good food makes the work seem bearable!

Jesus just fed the people a meal of fish and bread. That doesn't do much for my palate, but if I had not eaten all day, it would surely taste good. Jesus had offered the people a simple meal but one they really needed, and it impressed them so much that they followed him. Then he told them there is a greater food than the earthly fish and bread they received earlier from him. He explained that this bread would never perish. It is eternally present for those who would eat.

How confused the people must have been. They wanted another free meal and Jesus offered them heaven. They were focused on concrete, hold-it-in-my-hand food, and Jesus offered the Bread of Life. They could not make the leap from bread to bounty, from immediate gratification to lasting fulfillment.

The bread that Jesus offers may defy our ability to comprehend, yet we need to be aware of our hunger, so that when we are fed we will know beyond understanding that this is the food that counts. As hard as it may seem to believe, there really are times when we can forget about our bodily desires. These are the times when Christ's food fulfills our deepest desires, and we know that nothing else really is important.

Questions for Reflection

• What is the greatest source of nourishment for my soul?

_____

_____

_____

• Who feeds my spirit? How do I feed the spirit of others?

_____

_____

_____

Prayer

Lord, too often I find contentment in the creature comforts of this world. Help me see the deeper meaning of peace, and the fulfillment which can only be found in you. Let my soul taste your bread.

Third Tuesday of Easter

"I see the heavens opened and the Son of Man standing at the right hand of God!" But they covered their ears,...dragged him out of the city and began to stone him.   **Acts 7:56–58**

Someone had to speak so boldly about the truth of Jesus that folks would not be able to listen. And when he did, the righteous people had to silence the audacious voice of this man Stephen. After all, it was their duty to safeguard their religion from the radical elements in their midst.

If we listen closely we might be able to hear the voices of freedom singing about the glory of God today. These voices belong to the heralds of Good News who found that their love of Jesus was greater than their love of earthly life. From the early days of the Roman empire through the dark ages and reformation, then to the shores of our own land, the singing has continued. Even if the words vary, the proclamation is always the same: Jesus lives and is Lord!

Those who sing the Good News are the ordinary people who speak in an extraordinary fashion about the power of God. They live committed to something beyond the normal vision of the world. They see God and the Son of Man in the eyes of their neighbor. They can look beyond the surface and find the core of truth even in the difficult times.

When these singers need to sing out, watch the reaction of the people around you. Many of them might not physically kill the heralds of Good News, but they will surely try to kill the Spirit. Ah, but listen, the song is still being sung, isn't it? The truth will continue to be proclaimed, for the voices of God's triumph can never be silenced.

Questions for Reflection

• Which singers of salvation in our world are facing persecution?

_____

_____

_____

• How does my voice blend with those of the martyrs?

_____

_____

_____

Prayer

I want to dance to the songs that have been sung by saints of the past and saints in the present. I want to be one of your singers, too. Spirit of truth, direct my words and actions so that my song is in perfect harmony with you.

Third Wednesday of Easter

The crowds with one accord listened eagerly to what was said by Philip, hearing and seeing the signs that he did. So there was great joy in that city.   **Acts 8:5–6, 8**

When the time, the motivation, the right teacher, or other essential elements are in place, amazing things can happen for both the teacher and student. Perhaps the same can be said for the people of Samaria as well as Philip. Philip, a former tax collector went to preach the saving message of Jesus Christ. Movement took place in everyone involved in this story. The Spirit sailed into the burdened world of Samaria, and great joy erupted. The people took to heart the words of Philip, and there was dancing in the street.

We might imagine that Philip was surprised. Remember, however, that Philip was a Pentecost man! Philip was filled with the energy and the confidence of the Spirit. People strongly compelled by God are not surprised by much since everything is possible in Christ Jesus. On the other hand, the people of Samaria were surprised and overjoyed, for this was a new Spirit to them. They were hungry for the spiritual food Philip had to offer. They may not have known the words to express their hunger, but they knew when it was satisfied.

Many of us today speak of our love of God, but do we have the power to hold the attention of the hungry world around us? If the Philip inside us lacks motivation, then perhaps we need to get in touch with the Samarian who also dwells within. Perhaps we need to become conscious of the words and deeds of the Spirit-filled people around us, and let them enflame us once again.

Questions for Reflection

• Is the light of Christ shining brightly inside me or is it dull?

_____

_____

_____

• How thirsty am I for the new life of Christ?

_____

_____

_____

Prayer

I am Spirit-filled but still hungry. I sometimes overflow with the joy of a confident disciple, but at other times I lack the energy to kneel in prayer. Jesus, help me once again to find your Easter Spirit in my heart.

Third Thursday of Easter

Philip ran up to the chariot and heard the man reading the prophet Isaiah. Philip asked, "Do you understand what you are reading?" He replied, "How can I, unless someone guides me?"

Acts 8:29–31

I can remember driving through Fort Wayne, Indiana, one gray afternoon. I was not familiar with the streets, but I knew I wanted to go west. I hate to ask for directions, yet had I done so as soon as I had some doubts, I would have saved myself a great deal of time. What if someone like Philip had come up to me and said, "Are you lost? Do you need directions?" I am not sure how grateful I would have been.

How amazing that the more we think we know, the less open we are to actually learning more. In this reading from Acts, however, we find a person who was searching for more, who was inquisitive and thirsting for understanding. He readily invited Philip to offer some insight, and by the time they finished their conversation, the Ethiopian knew that he had found what he was looking for. Sometimes, someone comes into our lives for just a brief moment, yet we never forget what they had to tell us. We are forever changed because of their words.

Insight may come from an old man in the parish; it may be in the words of a peace demonstrator; it may come in a casual conversation with a coworker, or in the spoken observation of a small child. Those who seek understanding don't care how the word comes, but they will be very aware of the truth that is spoken. It will resonate in their soul. Those in touch with their inner being will know when the instruction is life-giving, when the instructor is from God.

Questions for Reflection
• How open am I to receiving instruction?

_____

_____

_____

• Am I willing to learn more about my faith?

_____

_____

_____

Prayer
Lord, teach me to listen for the small voices of your Spirit. May I learn to quiet my soul in prayer, so I will be able to pick out your message even when the world around me clamors for my attention.

Third Friday of Easter

Ananias laid his hands on Saul and said, "Brother Saul, the Lord Jesus, who appeared to you on your way here, has sent me so that you may regain your sight and be filled with the Holy Spirit." And immediately something like scales fell from his eyes, and his sight was restored. **Acts 9:17–18, 20**

Saul was ruthless in his pursuit of the followers of Jesus. Without a backward glance, he systematically went about arresting men and women who had embraced the message of Christ. The leaders of the Jewish community loved this man because he was willing to actively do something about this mushrooming new sect.

But a strange thing happened on his way to the toward Damascus. Saul fell to the ground. This shouldn't have been a big deal, just a bump in the road. All he had to do was get back up. Instead, Saul could not resume his old journey because he was blinded. He heard a voice speaking to him that frightened and confused him. Sure-of-himself Saul was now sure of nothing.

Ananias then came to pray over Saul. Amid all his confusion Saul's sight suddenly returned as if scales were falling away from his eyes. Saul saw the world around him with new eyes, especially the world inside himself. He could see his past for what it was, saw that his future would be forever changed, and he saw clearly from the heart his present reality in the light of Christ. When Saul got up again, he would have a new name, and he would be headed in a whole new direction.

Whichever way we are traveling, we need to be prepared to meet the Lord. If we are open to the Spirit, even when we fall the voice and the direction of God will be uncovered.

Questions for Reflection

• Have I ever experienced a painful fall that has led to a better life?

_____

_____

_____

• Who are the healers in my life, those who help me see clearly?

_____

_____

_____

Prayer

Jesus, help me know that when I fall, it is not the end of the story but the beginning of a new chapter. If I am confused by this new direction, give me the patience to wait for the scales to drop from my eyes.

Third Saturday of Easter

"The words that I have spoken to you are spirit and life. But among you there are some who do not believe. For this reason I have told you that no one can come to me unless it is granted by the Father." Because of this many of his disciples no longer went about with him. **John 6:63–66**

"You know, son," the father said on the day the boy's baseball team lost the big game, "you win a few, you lose a few." Life is like that, isn't it? Sometimes things go in our favor, but sometimes they do not. Sometimes we get in the middle of a venture, and circumstances force us to scuttle the project. Sometimes we give up on our dreams before they even have a chance to become reality.

As Jesus watched the disciples walk away from him, he must have been saddened that he had lost those followers. Perhaps he felt that those who left him had lost even more. Jesus knew those followers were good people, sincere people who were searching for a deeper meaning in their life. Yet some of the essential truths about the faith were hard for them to swallow.

We are fortunate to be Christians some two thousand years after the time of Jesus. We have a history to fall back on; we have traditions that have enriched our lives and we have witnesses that support the message of Jesus. We accept that Jesus is the truth, and we believe the Father has called us to follow his Son. Still the question remains, "Are we in the game?" If we live in such a way that we allow the Spirit to move in us and through us to bring life to the world, then we are part of the communion of Christian saints, a team with a very proud tradition.

Questions for Reflection

• Are there times when I choose not to "show up" for the work of being Christian?

_____

_____

_____

• How have I transformed personal losses into great victories?

_____

_____

_____

Prayer

Lord, help me to know that being a part of your team isn't about wearing the same uniform as everyone else or about being the most successful player. Help me know that even a living Water boy or girl is essential.

Fourth Sunday of Easter

"The one who enters by the gate is the shepherd of the sheep. He calls his own sheep by name and leads them out. When he has brought out all his own, he goes ahead of them, and the sheep follow him because they know his voice." **John 10:2–4**

In the 1990s, I had the opportunity to care for a small flock of sheep. One of the first sheep I had was extremely wild and frightened. I tried to befriend her but she would not come near me. Then one day I was out in the pasture with the sheep, waiting for a few visitors. When they arrived, this same frightened sheep came up and leaned against my leg, choosing to stay close to the one voice she knew. From that day on I only had to call out to her and she would come running.

In the gospel reading this Sunday, Jesus uses the image of the shepherd. He tells us that he leads his flock and they follow him because they recognize his voice. Implied here is the importance of voice recognition. His sheep can tell the difference between the voice of the one they can trust and the voice of a stranger. His sheep know he will never let them down.

In our personal struggles, or in the brutal events of nations at war, or even within a church in crisis, we have to be very attentive to the voice of Jesus. We need to listen with the ears of faith to hear the song of love and resurrection the shepherd sings for us. Listening to him daily helps us hear his voice amid all the other voices that clamor for our attention. Once we hear his voice, we are able to follow. We keep our eyes focused on the One who will lead us to safe pasture.

Questions for Reflection
• Which voices make it difficult for me to hear the shepherd?

_____

_____

_____

• Recall the first time I clearly heard Jesus' voice. What has helped me recognize him in more recent encounters?

_____

_____

_____

Prayer
I listen for your voice, Lord, but sometimes there is so much clatter around me and inside me that it is hard to hear you. Help me rise above the useless racket so I can hear your heart song.

Fourth Monday of Easter

The Holy Spirit fell upon them just as it had upon us at the beginning. If then God gave them the same gift that he gave us when we believed in the Lord Jesus Christ, who was I that I could hinder God?

Acts 11:15–17

The Spirit-filled Peter speaking here is no longer the man who was always vying with others for Jesus' attention. In this account from Acts Peter was relating to his friends how he came to understand that those who were baptized in the Spirit should not be hindered from spreading the word of God. "After all," Peter said, "if God has given them the gift, I will not get in the way."

This was a difficult hurdle for Peter to overcome. Peter was, after all, a man who had lived his whole life believing that a good Jew followed certain rules. But once Peter broke through the narrow confines dictating that only certain people, living certain ways, could follow Jesus, then Peter was able to see that faith in Jesus was meant for all people. The only qualification was the presence of the Spirit. If the Spirit was the prime motivator, nothing Peter could say or do would stop it anyway.

What are the narrow confines we try to wrap the Spirit in? Can the Spirit speak through anyone? Think about the subtle and overt ways that we try to harness the Spirit. Some of us can only accept the priest as primary spokesperson for the word of God. Some of us think the Spirit works only through the Catholic Christian community.

Look to Peter. What would he say?

Questions for Reflection

• How do I try to box the Spirit into my narrow world?

_____

_____

_____

Which persons do I find difficult to accept as they are?

_____

_____

_____

Prayer

My Jesus, I realize I have limited the scope of my horizons of faith. I exclude certain people because they don't fit my image of a Christian. Liberating Lord, widen and soften my narrow viewpoint.

Fourth Tuesday of Easter

Now those who were scattered because of the persecution spoke the word to no one except Jews. But among them were some men of Cyprus and Cyrene who spoke to the Hellenists also, proclaiming the Lord Jesus.　　　　**Acts 11:19–20**

At one time or another, most of us have felt the urge to engage in an activity that may shock others. We may not actually follow through; then again, we might feel compelled beyond our own understanding and simply do it.

Perhaps the first conversion of the Greeks was a similar situation. The Christians from Cyprus and Cyrene simply couldn't contain the joy, the energy, and the movement of the Spirit. How could these men hold the love of God to themselves when they were bursting to share it? And once the Greeks began to accept Jesus as Lord, who was going to halt the movement? Those disciples opened the doors to the world at the urging of the Spirit.

In the present-day church is the Spirit still living in our midst? Is the Spirit still pushing the envelope of our orthodox belief systems? The answer to these questions must be yes. If the Spirit is living, the Spirit will impel us to get up once in a while and dance in the aisles. The Good News demands the unexpected. The unplanned will occur so that life might be born in hearts that are hungry.

There will be struggles with those who would want to reign in the Spirit, but eventually they will lose. Even if it takes many years to accomplish, eventually the Spirit-filled community will pick up the beat and dance.

Questions for Reflection

• Have my actions ever been spontaneous, led by the Spirit?

_____

_____

_____

• What are some new movements of the Spirit that the Church as a whole has not accepted yet?

_____

_____

_____

Prayer

Spirit of Truth and New Life, never let me stand in the way of fresh winds of your love. May I risk the ridicule of those around me in order to dance in your freedom.

Fourth Wednesday of Easter

"You did not choose me but I chose you. And I appointed you
to go and bear fruit.... I am giving you these commands so that
you may love one another."   John 15:15–17

One of the great gifts in life is to have someone we trust, someone with
whom we can share our deepest longings and most intimate thoughts.
We consider ourselves truly blessed to have this person in our lives. A
fortunate married couple may find that gift in each other. For someone else it may be a parent or brother or sister. For some it is the kid
next door who remains our lifetime friend. These treasured relationships make all the difference during times of struggle and grief. We
know we can depend on them to be there for us no matter what.

Jesus has offered us this type of intimate relationship. In one way
or another Jesus has let us in on all the important secrets of life. He
has given us insight into the heart of the Father. Are we ready for this?

To add to this concept of intimacy Jesus also lets us know we have
been chosen by him. Since God did the choosing, the choice was the
right one. We know that we are significant and there is a mission for
us. There need not be any second-guessing or doubts on our part.

Now Jesus asks just one thing of us, "Love one another." He has
told us we are special by offering to make us intimate friends. He
has told us we are handpicked to be disciples. We have the knowledge and the commission, now all we have to do is to live as if we
believe it. If we believe that these gifts are ours, then all we have to
be is love poured out for the neighbor.

Questions for Reflection

• What is the most significant gift my best friend has given me? Have I thanked this person for the gift?

_____

_____

_____

• Did Jesus make a good choice when he called me to be a disciple?

_____

_____

_____

Prayer

Lord, I thank you for all the special people in my life who have been your messengers of love. May I pass this love along to all who are looking at me in order to see your face.

Fourth Thursday of Easter

"Very truly, I tell you, servants are not greater than their master, nor are messengers greater than the one who sent them. If you know these things, you are blessed if you do them."

John 13:16–17

When I was growing up, one of my mother's favorite expressions was, "You're getting a little too big for your britches!" This inferred I or one of my siblings had done or said something we really didn't have permission to do or say. This kind of behavior can also happen when we move into a new job. The person who thinks he or she knows more than the boss will be taken down a peg or two, or they will find themselves out on the street looking for a new place of employment.

Jesus tells us the same thing here. We are given a lot of freedom in our mission as messengers of the Good News, but we need to remember who is "boss." We need to remember that the good works we are performing are being done for God's glory, not our own. The key is to be in touch with ourselves enough to honestly be able to tell if we do things more for God or for ourselves. It can get tricky, so we need to be conscious of our motivations.

We should understand what it means to be the slave or the messenger. It means there will be a lot of letting go along the way. Sometimes we won't even realize it until someone points out to us that we are operating for selfish motives. Other times we will catch ourselves in the process of calling attention to ourselves. We can spend a lifetime learning to accept the status we have been offered by God, but that's what lifetimes are for, aren't they?

Questions for Reflection

• When do I pretend to be more important than I am?

_____

_____

_____

• What triggers my need to be in control, to be in charge?

_____

_____

_____

Prayer

I thank you, Jesus, for being my savior even though at times I seem to forget who is in charge. Help me accept your correction when I get a little too big for my faith britches, for my deepest desire is to truly love you wholeheartedly.

Fourth Friday of Easter

"In my Father's house there are many dwelling places. If I go and prepare a place for you, I will come again and will take you to myself, so that where I am, there you may be also."

John 14:2–3

Recently I traveled some distance to spend a couple of days with friends. As I drove to their home I anticipated the good food and drink I would enjoy. I thought about the beautiful lake that would be close by, and how I would walk there in the morning. I thought of the time we would spend together, sharing about every topic imaginable. When you travel to visit good friends, anticipation is part of the total package.

Jesus understands this feeling. He really wants us to be with him forever. He wants to have everything ready for our arrival, and he will even come back and pick us up. He wants us with him! Beyond the ability of this gospel passage to give comfort to those who are bereaved, this Scripture also gives those of us still on the journey that delightful sense of anticipation. This reading offers us a sense that we are moving closer and closer to the finest of homecomings. As we move through life, this reading will always remind us that the best is yet to come, and that it is all right to feel a little giddy about it.

How deeply God longs for us to be with him forever. All that he does is in anticipation of our coming. This is the kind of reading we need to just meditate on, slowly and gently. Taste it like a rich, fine wine. Walk with it always close to your heart. Somehow it will make the fears and the struggles a little less threatening.

Questions for Reflection

• Reflect on what a good visit with a friend is like for you. What special gifts does your host or hostess offer you?

_____

_____

_____

• What barriers prevent me from believing God loves me this much? How might I hand them over to God to be changed?

_____

_____

_____

Prayer

God, I cannot comprehend the depth of your love. Yet I am humbly grateful for those graced moments when I glimpse your unconditional caring in the people and events of my life.

Fourth Saturday of Easter

"It was necessary that the word of God should be spoken first to you. Since you reject it and judge yourselves to be unworthy of eternal life, we are now turning to the Gentiles." **Acts 13:46–47**

Spring is the season for tornadoes in the Midwest. Frequently the swift changes in temperature and wind currents will spawn thunderstorms in the volatile spring environment, and occasionally a tornado will accompany the severe weather. Those who have spent most of their lives in "tornado alley" know how to be prepared.

Sometimes the Scriptures act as a "first alert" for our faith. In this passage from the Acts of the Apostles, we are told that if we reject God's word, we will find ourselves unworthy of eternal life. Furthermore, if we don't want to offer the Word of God the hospitality of our hearts, then the Spirit will move to those who *will* embrace the Good News.

We can become pretty complacent or narrowminded about our faith, and lose our sense of the tremendous expansiveness of God's love. We can be caught up in ritual and law to the point that we believe only what fits our idea of religion is part of God's plan. But the danger in living this way is that when the wind of the Spirit comes and asks us to reorder our lives, our thinking, and our belief systems, we may not be prepared. Instead of the breeze that refreshes and airs out our spiritual home, the Spirit becomes a volatile force that scatters our small world in every direction.

Will we continue to move and grow in our faith, or will we stand still and face the winds of destruction?

Questions for Reflection

• How rigid am I in my beliefs? Whom would I exclude from my life?

_____

_____

_____

• Are there aspects of our church that may be too inflexible? How does that stifle the Spirit?

_____

_____

_____

Prayer

Spirit of expanding love, help me rejoice in your surprising ways. Let me not be tempted to limit my vision or my love. May I see with your eyes the possibilities, not the problems.

Fifth Sunday of Easter

Thomas said to him, "Lord, we do not know where you are going. How can we know the way?" Jesus said to him, "I am the way, and the truth, and the life. If you know me, you will know my Father also."   John 14:5–7

Perhaps we are a lot like Thomas, worrying about the way to achieve the end result. So much of our time is spent rushing from this project to that project, from this holiday to the next, from graduation to retirement, and on and on. We don't spend a lot of time smelling the roses along the way because we have deadlines to meet. The Christ-of-the-moment flashes by us as we speed toward journey's end.

What Jesus seems to suggest today is that the journey, the way itself, is what's important. We will find the important truths of life if we take the time to see with eyes of faith. Life is going on right now, and Jesus will reveal it if we are attentive. We watch where we are going in order to be present to the moment, to the beauty, to the presence of God.

The way, the compass of love that guides us is always at hand. If we know the loving Jesus, then we can ascertain if we are on the right path, Christ's path. The truth, the pearl of great price, is not found on some distant coastland, or at the end of our earthly existence. We don't have to travel miles or spend hours on the road to find it. The truth of Jesus is in our hearts. The life, the grace-filled energy necessary for the daily seeker, is within our breath and within the Spirit of all creation.

Imagine if we lived our lives focused on this heart journey, instead of on deadlines that mark off a timeline in time and space.

Questions for Reflection

• Am I present to the goal or present to my journey?

_____

_____

_____

• Where or in whom do I see the Son?

_____

_____

_____

Prayer

Jesus, sometimes I really think I know you, and at other times I don't seem to have a clue. Regardless of how I feel today, help me remember that you are here in my heart, leading the way, sharing the truth, and giving me life.

Fifth Monday of Easter

In Lystra there was a man sitting who had been crippled from birth. Seeing that the man had faith to be healed, Paul said in a loud voice, "Stand upright on your feet." And the man sprang up and began to walk. **Acts 14:8–10**

Have you ever played with a magnet? Run the magnet by some metal pieces and watch as they literally jump at the magnet. Then, as you start to remove the metal from the magnet, you can feel the pull, the resistance. Within the magnetic field a bond is created that holds the metal to the magnet.

I imagine Paul and the crippled man were also caught in a kind of magnetic bond, a force so powerful that when it was acknowledged between the two men, a miracle occurred. Seeing the faith of the crippled man and knowing the Spirit was alive in himself, Paul could boldly tell this man to get up and walk. Their mutual faith in the Lord Jesus Christ drew them together.

When people of powerful faith meet other people of strong conviction, unbelievable things can happen. These events are rightfully called miracles, and they are all around us. They can be spectacular, like this miraculous cure of a crippled man, but we must not overlook the miracles that don't make the headlines. How many homeless shelters or soup kitchens had their origin because faith-filled people began to dream about ways they could make a difference for the poor in their city? Is that not a miracle of faith?

When we have the courage to look one another in the eye and talk about our love of Jesus, miracles will happen. We will begin to feel the mutual pull of faith.

Questions for Reflection

• What is it like to meet another person alive with the Spirit?

_____

_____

_____

• How could you add your spark of faith to a project for the needy?

_____

_____

_____

Prayer

God of my heart, give me eyes to see the ordinary miracles around me. Help me understand that even when I simply dare to look into the eyes of my neighbor with love, a powerful miracle has taken place.

Fifth Tuesday of Easter

When they arrived, they called the church together and related all that God had done with them, and how he had opened a door of faith for the Gentiles.   **Acts 14:27**

This particular passage of Scripture comes at the conclusion of what, for lack of a better term, could be called a travelogue. Paul and Barnabas are returning from a long and adventurous trip that has taken them far and wide preaching the message of Jesus. We can imagine the great joy of the people when they see Paul and Barnabas again. When they were told about the day Paul was stoned, and how everyone thought he had died, they must have been awed. They might have been puzzled when the disciples explained why they had preached the message to the gentiles, a group that had been previously excluded.

Do *we* take time to share with one another stories about God's activity in our lives? In order to freely do so, we have to believe we have something worth sharing. We have to overcome the notion that we might be boring our listeners. To share our faith we have to risk the rejection of some of those who hear our words.

Where would we be if the gospel writers had not written down their stories, or if the author of Acts hadn't taken the time to let us know about all the marvelous things that were happening in the early church? Who will write and tell the current stories, the recent history of the believers, if not us? We may not all be writers or great storytellers, but if we can at least tell those in our own household or our neighbors and friends about how God has worked in our lives, we will be strengthening the faithful followers of Christ.

Questions for Reflection

• What is the most powerful good news I have heard this year?

_____

_____

_____

• Is there a story inside of me I could be sharing with others?

_____

_____

_____

Prayer

Lord, I am so grateful to the pilgrims I have met on my journey to the kingdom. Their stories have fed my soul and fortified my step. Help me realize that my story might be just the grace my neighbor needs.

Fifth Wednesday of Easter

Certain individuals were teaching the brothers, "Unless you are circumcised according to the custom of Moses, you cannot be saved." Paul and Barnabas and some of the others were appointed to go up to Jerusalem to discuss this question with the apostles and the elders. **Acts 15:1–2**

This Scripture passage should offer us encouragement. Here are two groups of good people who were filled with the Holy Spirit yet engaged in heated argument about whether or not followers of Jesus should be circumcised. Being a Spirit-filled Christian does not necessarily mean persons won't encounter conflict and division!

Some of us like to dance around conflict because we don't want to embrace that particular partner. Others find conflicted situations stimulating, and can't wait to get out there and tango with their adversaries. Most people, however, know that conflict is simply a fact of life.

In Acts we have two sides with very different viewpoints concerning the importance of circumcision. One side felt that it was important to hold on to the sacred tradition of circumcision. The other side believed that this particular tenet should not exclude those who accepted the teaching of Jesus Christ but remained uncircumcised. Because they all felt strongly about their particular position, they may not have been able to clearly hear the voice of the Spirit.

Like the participants in the reading today, can we be open to inviting someone from the outside, someone who has a little more objectivity to help us come to some resolutions, or does pride and fear of embarrassment stand in the way?

Questions for Reflection

• How do I handle conflicts in my life? Do I seek help?

_____

_____

_____

• When I thrive on conflict, what happens to the people around me?

_____

_____

_____

Prayer

Jesus, I know you never said it would be easy, but conflict is so uncomfortable, especially when everyone involved is seeking good. Whenever possible help me become open to the heralds of win-win solutions.

Fifth Thursday of Easter

"As the Father has loved me, so I have loved you; abide in my love. If you keep my commandments, you will abide in my love. I have said these things to you so that my joy may be in you, and that your joy may be complete." **John 15:9–11**

If you have been following the daily readings this week, you may say to yourself, "Didn't I just read about 'abiding in my love' on Sunday and again on Tuesday?" Perhaps you even flipped back to check how many times this phrase has come up in the last several days.

Actually, each of the readings this week have come from different verses of the fourteenth and fifteenth chapters of John's gospel. For those of us looking for a new message each day, this repetition of theme may be a little frustrating. But perhaps this concept of Christ's abiding love is so important that Jesus wants to make sure we get the message. He wants us to go back to these verses more than once to make sure we find all the richness buried in these words.

Each day we walk on this earth is a new day. Who I was yesterday is not who I am today, or who I will be tomorrow. The beauty of our living Scriptures is that what I heard yesterday when I read this passage may find a deeper place in my heart today, and an even deeper home tomorrow. Each day there may be a little different emphasis offered by the evangelist, and maybe today will be the day I "get it."

Isn't it worth a second or third look? Jesus seems to think so. Think of it as dancing one dance after another with your favorite partner. As you move through the steps over and over again, it becomes second nature for you to abide in that embrace.

Questions for Reflection

• What has changed about me in the last twenty-four hours?

_____

_____

_____

• Is it easier or more difficult for me to be with Jesus today? Why?

_____

_____

_____

Prayer

Christ Jesus, may I face each day with excitement about the possibilities that will be presented to me. May I live with a sense of expectancy, a sense that today might be the day I will be overwhelmed by your love.

Fifth Friday of Easter

"No one has greater love than this, to lay down one's life for one's friends." John 15:13

Husbands and wives know it. Mothers know it. Fathers do too. Grandparents have known it even longer. They can all tell you that people can love deeply and strongly enough to lay down their life for those they love. What is striking here is that Jesus says it is *essential* to love that deeply. Disciples know what Jesus knows: true love means the willingness to sacrifice oneself for love.

We all know the stories of special people who have given of

themselves in extraordinary ways. Perhaps they have died for their faith, or spent their lives like Mother Teresa of Calcutta, serving the poorest of the poor. What we don't often realize is that house after house, street after street, city after city, people all around us are giving of themselves in perhaps less dramatic but no less extraordinary ways as well.

One of these hearty souls may dwell in our own home. Maybe we have taken their selfless spirit of generosity for granted for many years. Could it be your mom, who may not have wanted to cook supper every evening, or who sacrificed her time for your projects? Maybe it's your dad, who goes to work at the stressful job that isn't always very rewarding but provides a roof over your head? Maybe it's the child who lovingly cares for aging parents.

The Christian community is made up of heroes and heroines such as these. During this Easter season let's celebrate the witness they are for us.

Questions for Reflection

• Who are the unsung heroes and heroines in my life?

_____

_____

_____

• Am I one of these faithful servants of Christ? How do I know?

_____

_____

_____

Prayer

Risen Savior, there are suffering servants of your love in my world but sometimes I do not acknowledge them. Help me show them how much their sacrifices have meant to my salvation.

Fifth Saturday of Easter

"If the world hates you, be aware that it hated me before it hated you."

John 15:18

Make no mistake about the language Jesus uses here. He does not say the world will dislike us or that it will be upset with us. No, Christ says that it hates us, abhors us, and is totally bent on destroying us.

The world is not friendly to the presence of Easter people in its midst. Easter people are entirely too committed to a future full of hope. Easter people live in the present moment always attuned to their Savior, but they never live just for the momentary gratification the world offers. Easter people are not selfish enough, greedy enough or envious enough, for the likes of this world.

The world Jesus speaks of in this gospel passage is not the world of soil and water and air but of the deprived world of a self-absorbed culture. All one has to do is look around to see how the hateful world condemns itself. In subtle and not-so-subtle ways the world reveals its hatred of the Easter promise. The world will try to convince us that accumulation of wealth is power and that power is a sign of God's approval. The world will justify its actions by declaring its scientific progress or legal freedom, but to those signed in the blood of Christ these actions are often revealed as acts having evil intent.

The closer we live to Jesus, the more hatred will rear its ugly head. But we need to remember that *nothing* can come between us and the love of Christ Jesus, the Lord.

Questions for Reflection
• What are the obvious signs of hatred I see in the world?

_____

_____

_____

• What veiled signs of hatred have I experienced in my world?

_____

_____

_____

Prayer

Lord, I am your child but I live in a world that is drunk on hatred. May I always seek to live in your shadow, buffered by your peace and love. Let me in turn offer support to others who are trying to hold out against hate.

Sixth Sunday of Easter

"If you love me, you will keep my commandments. And I will ask the Father, and he will give you another Advocate, to be with you forever. You know him, because he abides with you, and he will be in you."   John 14:15–17

Every president, at least in current practice in the United States, is surrounded by advisors most of the time. These "wisdom figures" help the president make decisions concerning domestic and foreign policy, media control and campaigning, legal issues, and much more. When the president makes an important decision, you can be sure that his advisors have looked at it from every angle.

We too have our own personal advisor available to us. This Spirit of wisdom is present twenty-four hours a day, seven days a week. This advocate of our welfare never takes a vacation or a day off. How conscious are we of the Spirit's presence?

The people living in the Spirit of Truth are not motivated by popularity polls or favorable ratings. Followers of truth allow themselves to be protected by the secret service of enlightenment and understanding that this Spirit shares with them. Followers of Jesus are confident when they approach the supreme court of heaven because their Advocate has never, ever lost a case.

This same Spirit of Jesus is engaged all around us in our world today. No one is too insignificant and no crisis of faith too small that it goes by without a response. This Advocate has her sleeves rolled up and is bandaging the wounded, counseling the grieving, walking on the protest line, and running in any race for any cure that will bring healing to creation.

Questions for Reflection

• Think of three times you met Jesus today. How do you know?

• What's the latest piece of advice the Spirit has shared with you? Did you take it?

Prayer

Come Holy Spirit. Make your presence known in my heart. Give me your insight and counsel so my choices will reflect your will.

Sixth Monday of Easter

"When the Advocate comes, whom I will send to you from the Father, the Spirit of truth who comes from the Father, he will testify on my behalf." **John 15:26**

In any courtroom drama the defendant in the case hopes to have people who will take the witness stand and testify on his or her behalf. Perhaps the witness has pertinent testimony that will give evidence of the person's innocence, or is there as a character witness.

In this reading from John, Jesus tells us that the Spirit will testify for him. There could be no more powerful advocate than the Holy Spirit, yet isn't it difficult sometimes to figure out what the Spirit is saying? We may find ourselves asking if this is the true Spirit of God that is giving testimony, or a spirit of discord.

Certainly the evidence of the Spirit seems quite clear in the lives of the saints. These were people filled with the Spirit. The choices they made in life certainly verified God's presence. Then there are all the people who respond to the needs of their neighbors in times of disaster or crisis. These people, too, witness for the defense of Jesus, the Spirit of good in the world.

If we take time to hear the God who speaks to us in the secret of our own hearts, we will be able to discern the true Spirit in the world. The Spirit will testify that this is truly what Jesus would do in the same situation. Would Jesus choose war as a way to settle disputes? Is capital punishment the choice of the Spirit? How important are money, position, and power to the Christian? Honest answers to questions like these will help you know the heart and spirit of Christ.

Questions for Reflection

• Is the testimony of the Spirit hard for me to hear? Why?

_____

_____

_____

• Am I courageous enough to give testimony for Jesus?

_____

_____

_____

Prayer

Christ, let me not be fooled by false witnesses who claim that you are directing their action. Help me know you well enough on the inside so that I can recognize your action in the world around me.

Sixth Tuesday of Easter

"Nevertheless I tell you the truth: it is to your advantage that I go away, for if I do not go away, the Advocate will not come to you; but if I go, I will send him to you."   **John 16:7**

The first day of school for a small child can be traumatic, not only for the child, but for the parent who must let go. Yet look what happens after that initial "letting go" has taken place. The child learns to read and do math, how to solve problems and discover the world of history and geography. All of this happens because the father or mother left their child at school one day.

Jesus tells us that if he stays, then God's Spirit will remain in him. He will be able to preach and teach to those around him. But if he leaves the bountiful Spirit will be able to move freely, just as the wind blows wherever it desires. Thus Jesus ascends to heaven—doesn't he? The answer to this question must be yes and no. Jesus did leave us, but the Spirit whom he sent is always available to us. He teaches us the important lessons of faith and love. Jesus comes to us in a special way in the Eucharist, so we remember just why he came to earth.

The Spirit of God is active in our lives in all places and spaces. Like the good parent, the Spirit teaches in the privacy of our own hearts, in the quiet moments of our day. The Spirit also encounters us as we move about in the world at large. The people we meet, the places we visit, the visions we dream, and the ideas we put into practice are permeated with the Spirit of God. Are we aware of this Spirit?

Questions for Reflection

• How aware am I of the presence of the Spirit in my daily life?

_____

_____

_____

• Which people in my life have shown me the most lasting impressions of the face of God? Have I thanked them?

_____

_____

_____

Prayer

Spirit God, I believe you are always with me, but I often go through the day without being conscious of your presence. Help me be aware of your abiding presence even in my most active moments.

Sixth Wednesday of Easter

"Athenians, I see how extremely religious you are in every way. For as I looked carefully at the objects of your worship, I found an altar with the inscription, 'To an unknown god.'" **Acts 17:22–23**

The Athenians, it seemed, had a god to cover every facet of life. And so when Paul found the altar to the "unknown god," he saw that these people knew they didn't have all the answers. Using this altar to the unknown god as his point of reference, Paul was able to suggest that he knew this God and that he, Paul, was appointed to reveal God's existence to the Athenians. The fact that these people realized there might be more to God than they already knew, insured they would be open to the words of Paul as he proclaimed Jesus Christ.

Christians believe that Jesus is the Son of God and that his Spirit is alive in the world today. We believe that everyone is under the rule of this one God. But are we open enough to see the many faces Christ reveals to the world? Would Paul be able to speak to us about Christ today, or would our minds and hearts be closed to new possibilities?

Just as Christ graced the openness of the Athenians with the presence of Paul in their lives, so, too, Jesus desires to bless our openness. There is great richness for those who would receive a fresh, new word. There is more love and truth and beauty than we already know about, if we are open to accept it. The wisest people in the world are the people who know they don't have all the answers and are open to learning more and deeper truths. The Athenians were wise people. Are we?

Questions for Reflection

• What facet of my faith life has deepened in the past five years because I have been willing to learn something new about Jesus?

_____

_____

• What aspects of my life might God be nudging me to look at?

_____

_____

_____

Prayer

Too often, Lord, I confine your Spirit to my own narrow images. I fail to realize that you want to continually stretch my horizons. Today may I open my heart just a crack to allow a fresh wind to blow into my heart.

Sixth Thursday of Easter

Paul went to see [Aquila and Priscilla], and, because he was of the same trade, he stayed with them, and they worked together—by trade they were tentmakers. **Act 18:1–3**

Most of us think of the first leaders of the church as people who spent all their time preaching and teaching the word of Christ. With so much to do and so many people to reach the apostles surely didn't have time to work at a regular job. Yet here we find Paul working side by side with two other Christians at the ordinary craft of tentmaking.

Paul was a hardy man grounded in the love of Christ, just as a tent is made of sturdy canvas that can be anchored to the earth. Paul also knew the need to provide shelter for the stranger, the neglected, and the alienated. He was good at designing a tent that could be altered so the space of the Christian tent might be widened to include everyone.

Beyond the wonderful symbolism of Paul the tentmaker, however, is the simple message that working for our daily bread and proclaiming the message of Jesus are not mutually exclusive. In fact this Scripture passage seems to indicate that the followers of Jesus are hardworking and practical people. Spreading the word of God doesn't take place just after the workday ends or on the weekends. Sometimes we proclaim the message of Christ in our offices, factories, and institutions simply by our example of integrity and honest labor.

Many people will waltz in and out of our lives. Look very carefully, for there are dancers all around us who will never be in the spotlight, but who are grounded in their love of the Lord. Perhaps you will see the face of Paul the tentmaker reflected in their eyes.

Questions for Reflection

• Who are the common laborers of love who have touched my life?

_____

_____

_____

• How do I live my Christian faith in a practical way day by day?

_____

_____

_____

Prayer

Thank you, God, for the gift of work, for the labor of my mind and hands. May I always honor you in even the smallest of my tasks.

Sixth Friday of Easter

"So you have pain now; but I will see you again, and your hearts will rejoice, and no one will take your joy from you."

John 16:22

When a dancer stands on stage and hears the thunderous applause of an appreciative audience, it is indeed a heady experience. All the hard work, the long hours of practice, and the frustrations finally pay off. Regardless whether the dancer ever has another triumphant night, this one particular experience of success will never be taken away.

In this passage from John Jesus tells his friends that he realizes they are going through a painful time in their pilgrimage of faith. He knows it is difficult, but he doesn't want these beloved followers to lose heart. He assures them he will see them again, and no one will be able to take away the joy they will experience.

Once we have experienced God, really experienced him, we know a lasting joy. This joy has staying power. Having experienced intimacy with God, we realize no one can take it away from us. It is ours to treasure through life and beyond. Only two things will prevent us from knowing this joy. The first is doubt based upon our belief that life in this world has to be endured in darkness without any glimpse of heaven. This doubt allows no room for the lavish love of God that can sustain us through the hard times. The second hindrance is also doubt, but this time we doubt the importance or validity of the experiences of God we have been given. We close ourselves off to the long-term joy and assurance that these graced moments provide.

If we allow ourselves to experience the resurrected Lord and embrace the joy of the experience, our joy will never be taken away from us.

Questions for Reflection
• What doubts hinder me from experiencing the touch of God?

_____

_____

_____

• How have my encounters sustained me through periods of doubt?

_____

_____

_____

Prayer
Lord, may I know your presence so deeply that I will be forever changed. May I never doubt the importance of those times in my life when I have embraced the power of your Spirit. May your joy be my joy always.

Sixth Saturday of Easter

"I have said these things to you in figures of speech. The hour is coming when I will no longer speak to you in figures, but will tell you plainly of the Father."   **John 16:25**

When a small child asks his or her mother how babies come into the world, most parents will give the child only as much information as he or she can handle. This is not the moment to have a heart-to-heart talk with the child about the aspects of reproduction. A young child cannot understand the science of life.

In this passage from John's gospel, Jesus realizes that his followers are not able to understand everything he could tell them about God. He can only speak to them vaguely about who he is and how he knows the Father. So he gives them only the amount of information they need for the time being. Yet he tells them that at some point, he will be able to speak freely to them about the Father.

If our image of God at forty is the same image we had at ten years of age, perhaps we need to be open to a healthier image. If we see Jesus only as the ascended King of glory, perhaps we need to acquaint ourselves with the humble Jesus who walked upon this earth. This Jesus will show us his face in the eyes of the poor, the neglected, and in the bloody wounds of the children caught in the wars we wage.

Are we ready to learn more about our God? Are we mature enough in our faith to handle what we could not comprehend as children? If we are open, then God will willingly share more fully with us when the time is right.

Questions for Reflection

• How has my image of God changed over the years?

_____

_____

_____

• What revelation of God has been hardest to accept?

_____

_____

_____

Prayer

Your countenance has many facets, Lord, and I have encountered only a few. Create in me more powerful eyes for contemplating the many planes and contours of your face revealed in the world around me.

The Ascension of the Lord

While staying with them, he ordered them not to leave Jerusalem, but to wait there for the promise of the Father. When he had said this, as they were watching, he was lifted up, and a cloud took him out of their sight.   **Acts 1:4, 8–9**

The disciples were there during Jesus' three years of teaching and miracles, his arrest and crucifixion, the resurrection appearances, and now this, ascending from the earth and vanishing in a cloud. How much of this sort of thing can a disciple handle?

The disciples were lost in mystery. So many unanswered questions, so many awesome experiences, and nothing seemed as it should be. Fisherman, tax collectors, and prostitutes should have been at the bottom of the chain, not the top. Jesus was gone but the Spirit was coming back in his place. And who was this Holy Spirit they were supposed to await?

When we are overwhelmed by mystery, all we can do is wait for understanding. Our emotions need to settle, our hearts return to a regular rhythm; stillness becomes our greatest ally. Conversation with others helps us realize we are not alone in dealing with the mystery, but in the end it is prayer that opens us to understanding.

Jesus knew that his ascension would dazzle the disciples into utter confusion, so he told them to wait in Jerusalem for the Spirit of understanding. We too will need to be expectant in the waiting, for we know not the day nor the hour that our Pentecost will dawn.

Questions for Reflection

• When was the last time I was dazzled by mystery? Stay with that experience once again today.

_____

_____

_____

• Can we hear Jesus telling us to wait? Let this call reach the barren parts of our soul.

_____

_____

_____

Prayer

Waiting for your Spirit can be exciting and scary at the same time. Help me quiet my soul and let go of my expectations and concerns now. Lord, let your fire of new life find my soul peacefully waiting.

Seventh Monday of Easter

Paul said to the disciples, "Did you receive the Holy Spirit when you became believers?" They replied, "No, we have not even heard that there is a Holy Spirit." **Acts 19:1–2**

As Jesus was about to ascend to heaven, he told the disciples to wait for the coming of the Advocate. During this week of preparation for Pentecost, we indeed wait. But how comfortable are we with waiting? Waiting in line at the grocery store, waiting in a traffic jam, waiting for an important phone call, or just waiting for a particularly bad day to be over are usually not high on our list of pastimes.

Recall the question Paul asks today, "Did you receive the Holy Spirit?" To have received the Holy Spirit means that we have come to know the Holy Spirit as intimately active in our lives. When we are aware that the Spirit is working in us, through us, and around us, then we know we have freely received the Spirit into our hearts.

This week while you are waiting in line, in traffic, or for that phone call, use the time to recall the ways in which you have received the Holy Spirit. Think about the experiences throughout your life when there were clear indications of the movement of the Spirit. Take the frustration and irritation of waiting this week, and transform it into gratitude and grace. If we can do this all week, through all our waiting, we will celebrate the feast of Pentecost more intimately and with more gratitude than we might have ever thought possible.

Questions for Reflection

• Have I simply heard of the Spirit or do I know the Spirit?

_____

_____

_____

• How does recalling the abundance of my life invite the Spirit to act even more fully within me?

_____

_____

_____

Prayer

Jesus, thank you for sending your Spirit into my life over and over again. I know I would be lost without the gentle sparks of fire that ignite my heart in love. Help me always be sensitive to this Advocate of Love.

Seventh Tuesday of Easter

"This is my commandment, that you love one another as I have loved you. No one has greater love than this, to lay down one's life for one's friends." **John 15:12–13**

To love those around me as Jesus loves me often seems like an impossible feat. First of all, I don't really know many people well enough to say whether I could love them or not. Second, there are lots of people I know but don't particularly like, so loving them seems a huge task. Finally, even with the people I do care about, there are limits to what I'll do for them. So how can I say I will "lay down my life for them"? Surely such a thing is beyond my capabilities; after all, I'm not Jesus Christ!

Most of us will not lay down our lives in dramatic fashion like Jesus or the martyrs. We live day in and day out, laying down our lives in a thousand little ways. We sacrifice for our children so they can have adequate clothing and schooling. We let go of some of our desires for success in order to promote the success of our partner. We give our most valuable treasure, time, to volunteer for a worthy cause. We take in an aged parent and rearrange our lives around their needs. We stand up and face ridicule for significant social justice issues. There is no blood spilled, yet we are putting our life on the line.

Being Jesus' friend is not easy. It is not without pain and sacrifice. This extraordinary relationship takes us to places we would prefer to avoid, yet we tremble at the thought of losing it. In the little ways we respond in friendship to those around us, we see a glimmer of what Jesus is willing to do for us.

Questions for Reflection

• Do I really believe that Jesus would die for me? (Be honest now!)

_____

_____

_____

• Which people in my life have laid down their lives for me?

_____

_____

_____

Prayer

Jesus, sometimes it is so hard to see your face in my neighbor. Sometimes I don't want to respond to the needs of those around me. Give me the will to offer my time, my talents, and my presence to those calling out to me.

Seventh Wednesday of Easter

"Keep watch over yourselves and over all the flock, of which the Holy Spirit has made you overseers, to shepherd the church of God that he obtained with the blood of his own Son."

Acts 20:28–30

Every so often in nature catastrophic events can potentially change the lay of the land. An earthquake causes a river to turn back on itself for a short while. This backwash becomes a large, new permanent lake. A terrific ice storm prunes a forest of all the dying branches and weak limbs. A volcano erupts and spews ash for miles around, devastating everything, but this ash becomes the fertile new soil for the forests and plains of the future.

On Sunday, when we celebrate Pentecost, we will be celebrating the birth of our church, a new church, one that is constantly struggling to become more the church of Jesus. Perhaps more than at any time in our recent past we are in need of a Pentecost celebration, a renewal of the Spirit of church.

We are part of a crippled church, but we too are responsible for what goes on in our church. Maybe there have been times when we needed to speak up, but we didn't want to rock the boat. Maybe we haven't voiced a challenge when our church seemed out of step with the Spirit. Too often we have been apathetic. This time in our history calls us to be the church, calls us to be involved and active and committed. The labor pains of our church can be pretty painful right now, but the honesty of the struggle will bring joy in the morning.

Questions for Reflection

• What are my responsibilities as a mature member of my church?

• Am I willing to be a prophet in my parish, or do I want to just go with the flow?

Prayer

Lord, I am part of the body of your church. Help me be a productive and vital member. May I do all I can to insure that this community of believers will continue to birth new life in your Spirit.

Seventh Thursday of Easter

"Father, I desire that those also, whom you have given me, may be with me where I am, to see my glory, which you have given me because you loved me before the foundation of the world."

John 17:24

Since my parents have died, I have felt the loss most at times when I want to share with them something good that has happened in my life. I find myself saying, "Wouldn't Dad have enjoyed this?" or "Wouldn't Mom get a kick out of that?" I imagine what they would say, and can almost see the smiles on their faces.

When we love someone deeply, it is difficult to lose him or her. These are people we have known well. We loved them and would like to have had them remain near. We want them to share the good times with us and to know their comfort in our difficult moments.

The prayer Jesus offers today reflects that he, too, felt this human desire. He wanted assurances from his Father that these friends would be able to join him one day. Jesus wanted his friends to be part of the celebration and to actually experience this glorious life with him.

At times we have to read between the lines of Scripture in order to find these points of contact, these relational links. Sometimes they are hidden within the context of a teaching. In order to grasp and accept the teaching of Jesus, we would be well served to discover these relational touchstones. By knowing the human Christ we see the gift of our own humanity. Relating to this human side of Jesus can help us understand why he wanted to share his glory with us. After all, it is the kind of gift we would want to give to someone we loved, isn't it?

Questions for Reflection

• What, for me, have been important clues in Scripture about the human Jesus?

_____

_____

_____

• Why is it important to live reflectively in order to know Jesus?

_____

_____

_____

Prayer

Thank you, Lord, for sharing your human desires with us through your expressions of joy, sorrow, longing and even anger. May we come to understand that being fully human often means being one with you.

Seventh Friday of Easter

He said to him the third time, "Simon son of John, do you love me?" Peter said to him, "Lord, you know everything; you know that I love you." Jesus said to him, "Feed my sheep." John 21:17

What did Jesus have in mind when he asked Peter the question, "Do you love me?" Maybe he wanted Peter to remember the three times he denied Jesus in the courtyard. Maybe Jesus wanted Peter to go through this ritual as penance for his betrayal. But perhaps in this encounter, Jesus offered Peter the gift of healing.

If Peter needed anything at this time, it was to know in his own heart that he loved Jesus. He may not have been quite sure about that since his betrayal. Yes, he was happy to see that Jesus had risen. Certainly he was awed by all that Jesus was saying and doing since Easter morning. Yet Peter may not have been sure of his love for Jesus.

In his tender compassion for Peter, Jesus understood that for Peter to continue as a disciple, he needed to believe in himself, in his capacity to love. Jesus did not ask these questions because he needed to know. He asked because Peter needed to know. When Peter felt the hurt, the consequences of his betrayal, he regained his confidence in his ability to love Jesus.

Sometimes in our own life, the pain that accompanies an argument or misunderstanding is the clearest sign to us that "Yes, I really do love this person." This pain is a sign of caring beyond our own selfish interest. As Peter allowed himself to hurt, he was once again grounded in the sure knowledge of his love for Jesus.

Questions for Reflection

• Can I see the pain and hurt of love as gift?

_____

_____

_____

• Is my heart big enough to hurt for the world? Can I act out of that love? In what ways?

_____

_____

_____

Prayer

Jesus, I know that at times I doubt my love for you. When I feel the pain of my doubt and my betrayal, let me also realize that it could be a clear sign of the love I hold in my heart for you.

Seventh Saturday of Easter

Peter turned and saw the disciple whom Jesus loved following them. He said to Jesus, "Lord, what about him?" Jesus said to him, "If it is my will that he remain until I come, what is that to you? Follow me!"

John 21:19–22

A heart attack victim is brought into the emergency room. Nurses and technicians scurry to start IVs, hook up a heart monitor, and administer medications to impede further damage to the patient's heart. After recuperating, when the patient is back on his feet, the doctor begins to set up a plan for a new lifestyle for the heart attack victim. Now it's up to the patient to make healthy changes in his or her life.

We look at Peter in this Scripture reading and shake our heads. Will he ever change? There he was worried whether the disciple Jesus loved was going to suffer. Could it be that Peter is exhibiting jealousy yet again? We might find ourselves saying, "Same old Peter." It seems as if he is back at square one.

Peter is like our patient in the emergency room. He has just recovered from a serious attack of heart pain initiated by his betrayal of Jesus. With his soul reconciled thanks to Jesus' help, Peter was ready to get back into life. We can see that he picked up where he had left off, hoping that the disciple whom Jesus loved would not get ahead of him.

This reading tells us that Peter had moved from sadness and depression to engage in life again. While we might wonder if Peter would ever get it right, we now know that Peter was at least in a space where he could be open to receive a new spirit. Reconciliation does this for us. It moves us back into a position that offers us a clearer view of where to find life.

Questions for Reflection

• When I am reconciled with someone, do I experience freedom?

_____

_____

_____

• What does Peter tell us about how to receive the Spirit?

_____

_____

_____

Prayer

Jesus, like Peter, I suffer dis-ease in my heart due to my sins. Bring me the healing balm of reconciliation so I might begin to see more clearly the path of salvation in front of me.

Pentecost Sunday

When the day of Pentecost had come, they were all together in one place. All of them were filled with the Holy Spirit and began to speak in other languages, as the Spirit gave them ability.

Acts 2:1, 4

I was a miserable student of foreign languages. Suffice it to say that if the Holy Spirit had given me the ability to speak in "other languages," it would have to be something different from my high school Spanish!

As church we are all confirmed in the Holy Spirit and called to communicate the message of Jesus, which is simply this: God is love. The Spirit offers us many languages to accomplish this task.

• *The language of service.* This is a universal language everyone can speak and everyone can understand. The Spirit desires that we become fluent in this language and practice it a lot.

• *The language of example.* How I live my life speaks volumes to the seeker looking for the true path of Christ.

• *The language of nonviolence and peace.* Sometimes we think we know this language well, but when we need it the most, we revert to words of defense and aggression. When this occurs our inner peace is lost and our world sees history repeat itself.

• *The language of presence.* This language speaks eloquently without a sound. It is especially helpful to those in need of comfort and who need someone to be with them as they face their last hours on earth.

• *The language of nature.* Living in harmony with our earthly home expresses our gratitude to God for his gift of sustaining life.

Final Reflection

• As we envision the effects of pentecostal language, can we let the Spirit's words become our primary language?

_____

_____

_____

Prayer

So often I find it difficult to speak the words of love to the world around me. Holy Spirit, fill the heart of this faithful pilgrim so I might converse in the languages that speak of your power.